DRAMATIC ACTS

A Guidebook to Making Meaning in the Theatre

Preliminary Edition

Rebecca Morrice
Colleen Reilly, Editor
David Skeele
Laura Smiley
Slippery Rock University

Kendall Hunt
publishing company

Cover image © *'Tis Pity She's a Whore*, directed by David Skeele for the Slippery Rock University Department of Theatre, 2005

Kendall Hunt
publishing company

www.kendallhunt.com
Send all inquiries to:
4050 Westmark Drive
Dubuque, IA 52004-1840

CONTENTS

SCOPE AND SEQUENCE

The objective of this text is to provide an introduction to the definitions, processes, and styles of theatre. Theatre is a medium of expression that has many meanings for multiple cultures, communities, and historical contexts. It is also a professional industry that contributes to the economic, social, and artistic climate of contemporary society. This text will outline the methodologies of Attending and Making theatre as it relates to you as an undergraduate in a liberal arts curriculum, a member of a campus community that celebrates the arts, and a citizen of the world.

The study of theatre at Slippery Rock University is focused on providing an understanding of its vital and necessary role in any society. Throughout this text we will examine the process of making meaning in the theatre. We will explore the strategies through which theatre practitioners communicate their vision. To achieve this we must look back at historical theatrical movements as we look forward to emerging theatrical practices. Our inquiry will be guided by the scholarly and professional experiences of the SRU theatre faculty and their collaborators.

ABOUT THE AUTHORS

Rebecca Morrice, MFA, received her BA in History of Art and Architecture from the University of Illinois at Chicago, and her MFA in costume design from the University of Illinois at Urbana-Champaign. She has designed costumes for theatre, dance, and opera, and has worked with a wide variety of theatre companies including American Players Theatre, CENTERSTAGE in Baltimore, Illinois Repertory Theatre, Geva Theatre, and Unseam'd Shakespeare. She is currently a member of the faculty at Slippery Rock University where she teaches costume design and technology, stage makeup, theatrical design history, and stage management.

Colleen Reilly, PhD, MLIS, MA: Since 1991 Colleen has served as an Arts Educator, Arts Administrator, Company Manager, Stage Manager, and Dramaturg for numerous organizations including Charleston Stage Company, the Spoleto Festival U.S.A., Children's Theatre of Charlotte, Opera Carolina, Pandora's Box, and Theatre 99. Each year she serves as the Festival Manager for the Piccolo Spoleto Fringe Festival at Theatre 99, which sees as many as 10,000 patrons in 16 days. She holds a PhD in Theatre History and Performance Studies from the University of Pittsburgh, where she also earned an MLIS in Archival Studies. She serves on the Executive Board of the Theatre Library Association, and has archived collections from the Yale School of Drama and the Historic Pittsburgh Project. She teaches classes in theatre history and dramatic literature, and leads the curriculum in Arts Administration at Slippery Rock University where she also serves as the Director of the Kaleidoscope Arts Festival.

David Skeele, PhD, MFA, MA, teaches playwriting and acting and directs productions at Slippery Rock University. His SRU productions include *Tallgrass Gothic, Jesus Christ Superstar, Cymbeline, Hedda Gabler, Pericles,* and *'Tis Pity She's a Whore.* David's original plays have received professional and collegiate productions in Los Angeles, Pittsburgh, Cleveland, Columbus, Omaha, and Orlando. Recently, SRU produced several of David's plays of supernatural horror—*Dark North, The Margins,* and *Deepchurch Hollow*—and brought them to the Edinburgh Festival Fringe in Edinburgh, Scotland, where they each received coveted five-star reviews. His horror novel *Raised In Darkness* is available on Kindle from amazon.com.

Laura Smiley, MFA, is an associate professor of theatre at Slippery Rock University. She teaches a variety of performance classes including Fundamentals of Acting, Directing, Auditioning Technique, Voice and Movement, and Acting Shakespeare. She has directed numerous performances for Slippery Rock Theatre, including *Fat Pig,* which was invited to perform at the American College Theatre Festival in 2011, and *Deepchurch Hollow,* which performed at the Edinburgh Fringe Festival, Scotland in 2010. Other recent SRU projects include *The 25th Annual Putnam County Spelling Bee, The Old Man's Wings, Inspecting Carol, Cabaret,* and *As You Like It.* Smiley is the artistic and executive director of the Unseam'd Shakespeare Company which she founded in 1994. Along with acting and directing in the Pittsburgh area, she has taught acting, voice, and movement at many area universities, including Point Park University, the University of Pittsburgh, and the Indiana University of Pennsylvania. In addition to many roles with Unseam'd Shakespeare, Laura has performed for the Pittsburgh Public Theatre, City Theatre, Starlight Productions, and her one-woman show, *Building*. She has guest directed for Living Images Arts in NYC, Bloomsburg University, and Indiana University of Pennsylvania, as well as for collaborations with the City Theatre and the Pittsburgh Chamber Music Society. She received her BFA in Acting from the Catholic University of America, Washington, DC, and her MFA in Acting from the University of Pittsburgh. She is a member in good standing in AEA, SAG, AFTRA, and the SAFD.

ATTENDING THEATRE

Colleen Reilly

Theatre is an art form that occurs under the unlikeliest of circumstances, and yet it has been practiced since the earliest formations of civilization. In its most basic formation, theatre requires the creation and presentation of an action in the presence of an audience collected in a particular space. There are four fundamental elements of theatre.

1	PRACTITIONER	A theatre PRACTITIONER is anyone who contributes to the making of theatrical art. As a fundamental unit of theatre, the PRACTITIONER refers to the presence of a live performer presenting an action.
2	ACTION	Aristotle defined drama as the "imitation of an action." As a fundamental unit of theatre the ACTION refers to that which is being dramatized or performed; i.e., what is the PRACTITIONER doing?
3	THEATRE	As a fundamental unit of theatre, the term "THEATRE" refers to the space in which the PRACTITIONER presents the ACTION. The THEATRE may be a traditional performance space or a space adapted for performance.
4	AUDIENCE	The presence of the AUDIENCE is the defining feature of theatrical art. The "liveness" of the theatrical event is what distinguishes it from other art forms.

Simply stated, for theatre to occur a PRACTITIONER must perform an ACTION in a THEATRE in the presence of an AUDIENCE.

Theatre practitioners will be discussed at length in the next section of the text, "Making Theatre." While many of you may be interested in the craft of the theatre, here we will discuss the role of the public sector in theatre arts through a discussion of Audiences, Theatre Spaces, and Performing Arts Organizations. Who is in the audience? What trends impact audience participation in the arts? Where do we attend theatre? How do these spaces inform theatre experiences? Who provides the resources to support theatre as an art form? We will explore these questions, create a common vocabulary, and invite you to think of the social implications of theatre in your communities.

THEATRE AUDIENCES

Colleen Reilly

CHAPTER OBJECTIVES

- To recognize theatre as a social transaction between practitioners and audiences.
- To cite the factors that contribute to active and passive audiences.
- To define aesthetic distance and consider its relationship to theatre.
- To understand the expectations of theatre etiquette.
- To define audience development and to understand many of its challenges.

KEY TERMS

Aesthetic Distance
Audience Development
Box Office
Groundling
House
Soliloquy
Theatre Etiquette

I want to begin by considering the role of the audience in the process of making meaning in the theatre. If we think of "theatre" as a cycle of choices being made by playwrights, directors, designers, actors, and producers, we can think of the audience as the conduit for that cycle. Theatre is by nature a social transaction. As American filmmaker, actor, theatre director, and screenwriter Orson Welles once said, "I want to give the audience a hint of a scene. No more than that. Give them too much and they won't contribute anything themselves. Give them a suggestion and you get them working with you. That's what gives the theatre meaning: when it becomes a social act." (Collier's, 29 January 1938.)

The social act of theatre is what makes it stand apart from other art forms. The presence of the audience is the defining feature of theatrical art. The social transaction of theatre cannot occur without an audience. The word "audience" means several different things, such as (1) a group of spectators at a public event, and (2) the *act* of hearing or attending to words and sounds. Let's take a moment to consider this distinction. In the first description the audience is a passive collective of individuals who are required to observe an event. The second description refers to an active process of engagement. The tension between an active and passive audience defines current trends in studying audience behavior.

Active Audiences

Historically, audiences have much more actively participated in the social transaction of theatre. We can trace the origins of the theatre that we practice to fifth-century BC Greece where part of the civic identity of the populace was defined by their attendance at and participation in an annual playwriting competition. Citizens actually campaigned to be elected as judges for the dramatic contest, and were vocal about their opinions about the performance. The audience comprised all levels of the social order from state and religious officials to possibly women and slaves, although scholars debate their participation. Everyone gathered for the communal religious and civic celebration of dramatic art. It transpired in the course of the day, and had a festival atmosphere that is sometimes forgotten in the solemn presentation of classical dramatic texts.

Roman audiences attended theatre alongside a wide spectrum of entertainments including mock battles, horse racing, exotic animal expositions and competitions, and generalized spectacles of violence. There is no evidence to suggest that their behavior was modified when faced with theatrical entertainments. In fact, it would appear that Roman practitioners faced many of the challenges of active audiences in what may be the first example of suggested theatre etiquette.

From the Prologue to playwright Plautus's *Poenulus* circa 210 BC: *Let no worn out harlot sit in front of the stage ... nor the usher roam about in front of people or show anyone to a seat while the actor is on the stage. Those who have had a leisurely nap at home should now cheerfully stand, or at least refrain from sleeping. Keep slaves from occupying the seats, there will be room for free men ... And let the nurses keep tiny children at home and not bring them to see the play ... Let matrons view the play in silence, laugh in silence, refrain from tinkling tones of chatter, they should take home their gossip...*

The Elizabethan public theatres where Shakespeare staged many of his plays in the sixteenth and seventeenth centuries were also festive environments. Theatrical presentations competed for audiences with cockfighting, bearbaiting, and other entertainments. Many of these occurred simultaneously just beyond the exterior of the outdoor playhouses. Inside these theatres patrons' admission could be gained for as little as a penny, but additional amenities such as a seat with a cushion or in a private box were as much as six times that amount.

BOX OFFICE

The box office is the location for ticket sales. The terms derive from Elizabethan public theatres where patrons dropped their pennies in a centrally located box which was then stored in an office offstage during the performance—thus the title "Box Office." Most contemporary theatres offer phone and online sales in addition to regular box office hours. Many times you must purchase your tickets directly at the box office in order to receive any discounts.

Nearly one third of the Elizabethan audience stood throughout the performance, and there is evidence that gambling, trading, thievery, and prostitution were rampant in the public theatres while the play progressed.

GROUNDLING

A spectator who stood in the yard or pit of Elizabethan public theatres. The term became slang for people of unsophisticated taste. In 1964 a comedy improvisation troupe in Los Angeles took the name and since has launched the careers of comedians like Will Ferrell, Lisa Kudrow, Kathy Griffin, and countless others.

French and Italian theatres of the Renaissance were equally divided between the entertainment on the stage and that provided by the audience interacting with the performance. While most plays were produced indoors, audience seating extended to chairs placed on the stage that could be purchased by the aristocracy.

This continued into the eighteenth century when theatre architecture emphasized the class divisions with seating available in the pit, gallery, and box. It is important to note, however, that none of the seating was fixed to the floor. Seats could be moved to accommodate a view of the stage or other audience members.

The experience that many of us take for granted in the theatre of assigned seating and darkened auditoriums is a relatively "new" way for audiences to interact with the stage. As recently as 100 years ago most theatres contained no *house lights* or controlled lighting for the audience. Audiences shared the illumination from the stage, and were active, sometimes to the point of being rowdy. They commented on what they were seeing to each other and to the performers on stage. They freely demanded that actors repeat **soliloquies**, and other poetic forms of dramatic texts. As in the definition of *audience*, they were engaged in the act of hearing and attending to words and had very high expectations for the performers.

SOLILOQUY
A dramatic speech through which a character reveals his or her inner thoughts and emotions. The most famous soliloquies are found in Shakespeare, such as Hamlet's *To Be or Not to Be.*

Audience seating on benches or free standing chairs could be rearranged at will. Tickets allowed patrons to gain entry to the performance, but did not require them to sit still or be quiet. If there was something occurring on stage that did not meet their standards, they would sometimes shout the performers off stage. Their evaluation of the performance ranged from expectations to how certain language should be delivered to the preference for a particular actor, much in the same way that we follow celebrities in the media and patronize their films, music, and Facebook pages.

My favorite example of audience behavior in the nineteenth century is the 1849 Astor Place Riot. Tensions were high in the Astor Opera House as English actor William Charles Macready took the stage for a performance of *Macbeth* on May 7, 1849. The top level of seating had been purchased by hundreds of supporters of actor Edwin Forrest, Macready's American rival. Macready was shouted off the stage after a barrage of rotten eggs, potatoes, and sundry other items greeted his entrance. He vowed to return to the more civilized stages of England but was persuaded to deliver a second performance on May 10. The militia was called to police the 10,000 people who arrived at the theatre to take sides on the Forrest-Macready divide. The crowd broke into violence and 22 people were killed.

While there are many factors that contributed to the escalation to violence over an acting quarrel—such as class warfare, friction between English and American cultural identities, and divisions across political parties—the reality that this quarrel took place in the theatre speaks to the dynamic cultural space that theatre occupied in the nineteenth century. We tend to think of the theatre now as a place for our most polite and formal behavior, but our roots as a national culture are embedded in a much more relaxed and democratized space.

Passive Audiences

How did we move from the pub-like atmosphere of the nineteenth century to the church-like theatre of the twenty-first? Two inventions of the twentieth century contributed directly to aligning theatergoers to the first definition of *audience* as a group of spectators at a public event.

1. **CONTROLLED LIGHTING**
2. **THE INTRODUCTION OF THEATRE ETIQUETTE**

Controlled Lighting

At the turn of the twentieth century theatres radically altered the theatergoing experience by making the transition from gas lamps to electrical lighting. Not only did this eliminate the noxious fumes that would have permeated the **house**, but also practitioners were able to begin to control audience behavior by dimming the lights over the audience and more brightly illuminating the stage.

HOUSE

The seating area for the audience. This term can also refer to the seating capacity and arrangement; i.e., how many seats in the house tonight? Or, the house is empty. The lobby or reception area is referred to as the Front of House and is staffed by personnel who coordinate with other theatre practitioners to facilitate the audience experience. These include the Box Office Manager, Box Office Staff, House Manager, and Ushers.

Audiences who were accustomed to seeing and being seen were guided toward a more passive experience of observation. Furthermore, the experience of sitting in the dark discouraged audience participation and conversation, making the theatre experience more personal and private.

Changes in the lighting of the house also contributed to more control of **aesthetic distance** for practitioners of theatre. Aesthetic distance is a strategy used by practitioners to affect an audience's emotional identification with the world of the play. Some performances demand that the audience become completely absorbed and invested in the circumstances of the play, in which case there is little aesthetic distance between the audience and the performance. Other performances require that the audience remain objective and aware that the circumstances of the play are radically different from their own reality. In this case there is extreme aesthetic distance.

When I saw *August: Osage County* on Broadway, I was completely drawn into the story and lives of the characters of this domestic drama. The play was three hours long but when the lights came up for intermission, I just wanted to see what happened next. This is an example of little aesthetic distance. When I go experience a Cirque du Soleil production, there is a magical world created that I am drawn to, but the experience is so extraordinary and full of spectacle that I am always reminded that I am watching a performance, one that I also enjoy. This is an example of great aesthetic distance.

—Laura Smiley

Another way to think of aesthetic distance is to ask yourself: to what extent am I being asked to believe the events I am watching are real? To what extent am I being reminded that I am watching a performance of something?

AESTHETIC DISTANCE
The degree of emotional connection or identification with a performance. Little aesthetic distance means that the audience feels very close and is absorbed in the world of the play. Great aesthetic distance means that the audience remains aware of a performance and/or is constantly reminded that the world of the play is a fictional construction.

The Introduction of Theatre Etiquette

Many of you may have had your first theatergoing experience through a school field trip to a matinee performance. It is likely that in preparation for this experience you were instructed by your teacher how to behave in the theatre, or at the very least, handed a program note or leaflet that outlined the expectations of your behavior. The development of **theatre etiquette** has had a profound effect on audience behavior since its introduction in the early twentieth century.

THEATRE ETIQUETTE
A system of prescribed behavior determined by cultural organizations to facilitate a positive experience for artists and audience members.

Scholars mark a shift in divisions between "Arts" and "Entertainment" in the turn of the twentieth century that corresponds with increasing class consciousness. They argue that the monied classes claimed the Arts, and left Entertainment to the rest of us. In order to regain access to the Arts we were asked to model the behavior of the upper classes, who prescribed a new relationship to attending performances. The active audience was silenced, and the relationship between performances and audiences became more and more reverential.

Over time theatre etiquette has become more relaxed, and faced new challenges as audiences have recommitted themselves to active participation. For many people that includes engaging with social media at all times to enhance and record their experience. However, it remains inappropriate to text, tweet, or update your Facebook status during a performance. This is not only a matter of etiquette, but also one of controlled lighting! Surveys reveal that the backlighting of electronic devices in a dark house is the single most cited distraction for audience and performers alike.

SLIPPERY ROCK UNIVERSITY THEATRE ETIQUETTE

While attending our performances we want you to relax, enjoy, and be yourselves. We also want to safeguard the experience for other patrons and for the many people who have worked hard to make this production a success. We recommend the following to optimize your experience:

1. Arrive on time. Late seating can be problematic due to lighting and safety concerns. It can also be a distraction to other audience members and the performers. In the event that you do arrive late, please cooperate with our house manager who will seat you at the first designated opportunity!

2. Turn off electronic devices. The sound and lighting can be distracting and/or dangerous to actors making entrances and exits under extremely dark conditions. The electronic signal can also interfere with our wireless technology and disrupt our technical processes.

3. Do not take photographs or use recording devices. We are bound by copyright law to protect the integrity of this performance and cannot allow unauthorized reproductions.

4. Complete the social transaction. Voice your responses after the performance through social media, community forums, and publications. Attend talkbacks, contact our department, and become involved.

Contemporary Theatre Audiences

The key to your participation at theatre events is to discover where your preference for audience participation falls on the spectrum between active and passive. There is no one-size-fits-all solution, but by accumulating audience experiences you will develop a better perspective on what kinds of performances you might enjoy. Theatre does not exist as a monolithic institution, and comes in many forms. In addition to the performances that you will be attending this semester, consider the following:

IF YOU LIKE:	THEN YOU COULD TRY:
Interacting with performers Commenting on performances	Improvisational Theatre
Spectacle Familiar story lines or songs	Musical Theatre
A relaxed atmosphere Dining during the performance	Shakespeare in the Park

Audience development has become an important consideration for many practitioners seeking to build, enhance, or attract individuals to participate in arts events. Professionals working in audience development identify barriers to attendance for potential audiences and address them by creating new points of entry, or ways that audiences can access arts experiences. Barriers to attendance can include, cost, location, and attitudes towards the arts.

AUDIENCE DEVELOPMENT

The goals of audience development are increasing awareness of, and participation in, the activities of arts organizations. Effective audience development is incorporated into the full range of an organization's activities, including programming, operations, marketing and public relations, education and outreach, and fund-raising.

The cost of tickets is often a barrier to attendance for many potential audience members, but there are ways to negotiate individual ticket prices. You can take advantage of volunteer programs, student discounts, or subscription packages.

THEATRE TICKETS

1. Volunteer: Many arts organizations, including the Slippery Rock Theatre Department, offer free seating to performances for which you volunteer to usher or assist with the front of house.
2. Single Ticket Purchases: Look for ongoing student discounts, or "rush" specials that allow you to purchase tickets at special prices on the day of the performance.
3. Subscriptions: You can sometimes save considerable money over single ticket purchases by becoming a subscriber, which means buying a package or "subscription" that includes tickets to several or all of a theatre's productions during a season. Many theatres offer "Flex Tickets" where you purchase a pre-selected number of tickets in advance, and can use them for any production of that theatre in the season, or within a designated time period.

Many theatres fail to attract new audiences because they do not extend themselves to a large enough geographic area. Where there is a high concentration of theatrical activity, in New York, Philadelphia, Chicago, London, and Los Angeles, for example, theatre districts emerge as destinations for locals and tourists alike to participate in arts experiences. They draw audiences large enough to sustain their theatrical activity. Cultural districts are often formed in areas where there may be the presence of multiple arts organizations, but less theatrical activity. Pittsburgh has a cultural district.

The Cultural District is home to Downtown Pittsburgh's dynamic art and entertainment scene. Discover a plethora of choices for live entertainment—contemporary music, modern dance, visual art and thought-provoking theatre, as well as classical music, opera, ballet, popular musical theatre, and more. http://www.culturaldistrict.org/

Cultural districts can reconcile location and attitudes towards the arts. The formation of cultural districts is often part of a larger process of urban renewal and re-vitalization. As residents are able to reclaim part of their urban landscape through theatres, galleries, and restaurants, they begin to experience the value of the arts in their communities. Cultural districts also allow organizations to share resources and audiences. They provide a kind of "one-stop shopping" for people looking for arts experiences.

Attitudes towards the arts are one of the largest barriers to participation that audiences and practitioners face. Interest in and access to the arts is tied to economic cycles of growth and decline. In periods of economic boom, consumers extend their largesse to arts participation and philanthropy. In periods of economic restraint, the institution of theatre faces debates over its value to society.

That perceived value is complicated by emerging forms of arts participation including live broadcast of performances to satellite locations, access to productions via social media, trends in personalized arts experiences through emerging technologies, and distribution of theatrical performances through 3-D movies. Practitioners in the theatre are exploring new methods to ensure the social transaction of the live event.

Human beings have gathered to share stories in every known society, and in its broadest definition we can see theatrical practice in every historical epoch. Over time theatre has served as a religious ritual, a political tool, a form of protest, and a celebration of humanity. We tend to think of these modes of performance as being disparate, but they often overlap. For today's society, theatre can mean many different things such as a physical space, a form of art and/or entertainment, and something tourists like to see in big cities.

The question, "Why attend the theatre?" is one that scholars, critics, and practitioners share with the theatergoing and non-theatergoing public alike. Historically, the practice of theatre has been a central function of civic life. The word "theatre" derives from the Greek expression *theatron* or "seeing place". For classical civilization, the theatre provided a public space to see, be seen, and to present dramatic action. Today theatre exists on the margins of many other "seeing" activities, including film, television, and social media. The next chapter will more deeply investigate the "seeing places" of theatre spaces.

Conclusion

Theatre is a social transaction that can only occur in the presence of the audience. Historically, the nature of that transaction has been extremely active as compared to the more passive role prescribed to today's audiences. Aesthetic distance plays a role in guiding audience behavior, as does training in theatre etiquette and traditional audience experiences. Audience development seeks not only to attract more audience members but also to create more active audience experiences. These practices emphasize the role of the audience in making meaning in the theatre.

Exercises

Obtain prior approval to attend a performance in addition to the two productions assigned. Prepare a 1-2 page description of the production that you attend that must contain the following. (Hint: Try to use language more specific than "good" or "bad.")

- Name of Play, Theatre, and Location
- Paragraph 1: A thesis statement that describes the idea of the play, or what you think it is about. No synopsis!
- Paragraph 2: Describe the choices made by the director, actors, and designers. Do they work? Why, or why not?
- Paragraph 3: Describe a scene from the play that supports your thesis statement and evaluation of the effectiveness of the theatrical choices. Make a conclusive statement.

THEATRE SPACES

Rebecca Morrice

CHAPTER OBJECTIVES

- Identify different types of theatre spaces such as arena, proscenium, and thrust.
- List features of theatre spaces from different historical periods.
- Trace the development of scenery through different historical periods.
- Recognize that different styles of theatre require different spaces.
- Locate current theatre architecture as a relatively new development in theatre history.

KEY TERMS

Corrales
Deus ex machina
Naumachiae
Orchestra
Proscenium theatre
Skene

Like many elements within our modern culture, the *building* you most likely occupy when attending your theatre course owes a great debt to the cultures that came before. Of the styles of theatre building common to the modern cultures of the Western Hemisphere (primarily the Americas and Western Europe), many elements can be traced all the way back to the ancient Greeks in the fifth and sixth centuries BC. Other elements were introduced during the medieval and Renaissance eras. In essence a modern theatre space is an interesting medley of ideas that have been forged together over time, most of which have been chosen specifically with the best interests of the audience—you—in mind.

> Look around a modern theatre building. What are some of the elements that you can recognize as being common to many modern theatres? Is it an *arena* theatre or *theatre in the round?* Is the stage raised up? Is there an area in front of the raised stage where an *orchestra* might be seated? Are the seats placed at an angle or *rake?* The Greeks were doing all of this at least two thousand years ago. Is there a curtain? The ancient Romans first did that. Is it a *proscenium* style theatre? Is there painted *perspective scenery?* Is the theatre indoors? These are all elements that were first introduced during the Renaissance, five to six hundred years ago.

Types of Theatre Spaces

We'll begin this section by introducing some of the most common types of spaces used in Western theatre today.

Arena theatre (aka *theatre in the round)* is a theatre space in which the audience surrounds the acting/performance space. This type of stage space usually allows the audience to sit closer to the action, but cannot make use of a lot of scenery because it would block the audience's view.

Proscenium theatre is a space in which the audience faces the acting/performance space and is usually separated from the actors by a *proscenium arch* which acts like a picture frame. This is the style of theatre space most familiar to audiences today. Is it also referred to as *theatre of the fourth-wall removed* because it reflects how watching a performance in this style is often like watching the characters inside a box that has had one side removed. It allows us to voyeuristically peer into their world—seemingly without them knowing we are watching!

Thrust theatre is a space in which the audience sits on three sides of the acting/performance space. This type of theatre space combines elements of the previous two, in that the three sided seating allows the audience to sit closer to the stage then they would in a proscenium style theatre and allows for more scenery than there could be in an arena format. For many modern directors, this style of theatre space is quite desirable in that it offers "the best of both worlds."

Other types of theatre spaces that you might experience as an audience member include:

Alley theatre which is a space that places a long narrow stage in between two long banks of seating. **Think of it almost like a tennis court with seating on either side of the playing space.**

—Laura Smiley

Environmental space, which has nothing to do necessarily with the outdoors, but instead is a type of theatre where the boundaries between where the audience exists and where the performers exist are blurred.

Found space, refers to a space that is not ordinarily a theatre, which was chosen for the performance because it provides the perfect location as it already is. **Quantum Theatre in Pittsburgh exclusively creates productions in found spaces. I saw *The Crucible* performed in the Rose Garden at Mellon Park. Director Roger Henderson says, "I wanted to explore the idea that nature has gone awry...and that not having walls does not prevent them from trapping themselves." There were wooden platforms built in various places in the Garden, surrounded by overgrown hedges and weeds; this for me signified how difficult it is to restrain nature.**

—Laura Smiley

A *black-box theatre* is an indoor space (it can be anything!) that is often painted black and has flexible seating and lighting positions. This type of theatre can be rearranged to create whatever configuration of space is best for the current production.

Historically, it is said that the first theatre spaces were *arena* or *theatre-in-the-round* spaces. Some say this is because humans are compelled to form circles, but really, the reason is much more simple. When there is something that a group of people want to see, the most logical way to approach that situation is to surround the thing you want to see—and this includes a performance. There is nothing more psychological to it than the need to see what you want to see. Thus, the earliest stage spaces were *arena* because it was the most logical solution for the audience.

Ancient Greece

Before they began building permanent theatre spaces, the ancient Greeks were using *threshing circles* to perform in. These were circles of land outside of the towns that were cleared for the purpose of threshing grain.

These round spaces found a second purpose when they weren't in use for threshing—they became performance spaces. The performer(s) would stand in the center while the audience gathered in the circle around them to watch. Eventually these spaces were paved with stone and were called the **orchestra** or "playing place".

Once theatre gained a more important place within the religion and culture of Greece, they began to locate these orchestras at the base of natural hillsides which also gave the spaces great acoustics and let the people carve seating out of the hill itself. At first these benches were made out of wood, and later, out of stone. Many of these spaces, once built, were in continuous use for hundreds of years and still exist today.

Of all of the theatres built by the ancient Greeks, one of the best examples to study is the Theatre of Dionysus.

First built around the sixth century BC, the Theatre of Dionysus began as little more than a paved threshing circle with a nearby temple dedicated to the god Dionysus. Because much of the theatre created by the Ancient Greeks was directly connected to their polytheistic religion, their theatre spaces often had an altar, a temple, or both associated with them. This allowed the audience members not only to enjoy the entertainment, but also to pay their respects to the gods at the same time. In many ways, attending the theatre in the ancient Greek world was a little like attending church.

At first, the orchestra at the Theatre of Dionysus was perfectly circular with the audience surrounding on all sides. As the complexity of the plays performed there increased, the need for storage spaces for the masks and costumes commonly used increased as well. This led to the creation of a building called a **skene**, which was placed on one side of the orchestra and was one or two stories tall. This effectively changed the *arena* style theatre into a *thrust* format with the audience sitting around three sides of the orchestra in a seating area known as the *theatron* or *cavea*.

Though related to our word *scenery*, the *skene* building was not originally intended as scenery. In fact, the Greeks, whose outdoor theatre spaces were at the mercy of the weather, made little use of scenery as we think of it. Instead they relied on the words of the playwright, the actors, and the imagination of the audience to set the location of their plays.

Once the *skene* was built, it was only a short while before the idea of creating a raised stage occurred to the Greeks. This raised stage not only allowed the audience to see the actors better, but also introduced the idea of physical levels of performance to the Greek theatre. One of the conventions of the Greek theatre was the use of a *chorus*. The chorus was a group of performers (usually between eight and twelve) who spoke or chanted in unison during the play. In many ways, the chorus was meant to represent the audience who, if ever confused about what they should be thinking or feeling about the characters or ideas in the play, could look to the words of the chorus for guidance. As the plays developed, there became more of a desire or need to place the regular characters of the play on the raised stage while leaving the chorus to occupy the orchestra which was more physically connected to the audience. The idea of levels was even taken a step further when Greek playwrights began using the roofs of the *skene* buildings as locations where actors portraying the gods could perform. A crane-like machine was used to lift the god-actors into place on the roof and even led to the term **deus ex machina**, or literally, "god in the machine," which is a term we still use today to indicate a sudden and unexpected ending or outcome to a plot.

Eventually, a *skene* building, the *proskenion* which was a low platform between the *skene* and the orchestra, and a raised stage were added to the Theatre of Dionysus. These began to encroach on the orchestra causing it to become more of a semi-circle. In fact, as time progressed and the use of the chorus began to diminish, Greek theatres saw the orchestra as less and less important. It eventually became little more than a sliver of the circle it once had been. Modern theatres still retain this feature in the area in front of the raised stage where the group of musicians (the *orchestra*!) is seated when performing for musicals and operas.

While the Greeks did not use a great deal of scenery, the archaeological evidence from the theatres suggests to us that there were at least two devices that may have been used for this purpose.

The first were *pinakes,* which were flat panels that were inserted into grooves in the openings of some *skene* buildings. These were removeable and may have been used in a similar way to how modern theatre designers use *flats.* The other devices were *periaktoi,* whose purpose is still debated by historians. *Periaktoi* were stone prisms several feet tall with a hollowed center through which a pole could be placed. Several of these *periaktoi* were then lined up together. When all the *periaktoi* were turned to display any of their three faces, they worked similarly to modern moving billboards or like the letters used on the original version of the television program *Wheel of Fortune.* The mystery that still exists is what was painted on them. While the stones themselves have been found at these theatre sites, the paint that was on them has not survived time and the elements. It has been hypothesized that they may have been used as painted scenery. But, because they are found to the sides of the orchestra rather than behind, where scenery would traditionally be placed, the more plausible suggestion is that *periaktoi* were used as a playbill or program of sorts. Since many ancient Greek plays were presented as a part of a play competition, it is entirely possible that the *periaktoi* had the titles of plays and the names of playwrights painted on them. As the performance moved from play to play, the faces of the *periaktoi* would be changed to keep the audience informed as to which play they were currently watching.

Ancient Rome

Ancient Roman theatres bear some strong resemblances to those of the ancient Greeks. In fact, many Roman theatres are actually remodeled Greek theatres. The Romans were well aware of the style of theatre space preferred by the Greeks and as they gradually became the predominant culture, they chose to adopt the Greek style of theatre but adapted it to better suit their needs. In the ancient Roman style of playwriting, the chorus was no longer an important element and, as such, the need for the orchestra diminished. In many Roman theatres, the orchestra was changed into seating for more privileged audience members. In others, the orchestra was surrounded by a barred-fence and animal fights were held there.

In Roman theatres, there became more of a focus on the building behind the raised stage.

While the Greeks called it *skene*, the Romans referred to it as a *scaenae frons* or *frons scaenae*—"scenic front"—which better reflects their more decorative approach to the building.

While still not exactly scenery in the modern sense the Roman theatre building has indeed become much more decorative with statues and columns covering it. The Romans are also credited with creating the first stage curtain, the *aulaeum*, designed to keep scenic elements from the audience's view until a certain time.

Unlike modern curtains, the *aulaeum* was usually lowered into a trough to reveal the view, rather than being raised out of the way.

The style of theatre architecture seen at the Theatre of Pompey in Rome was copied all over the Roman Empire. The Romans are well known historically for their advancements in engineering, which allowed them to build their theatres free-standing rather than carved out of hillsides. However, the people had more of a desire to watch gladiatorial combats and other types of entertainment than plays. To serve that desire, the Roman theatres often shared one wall of the building with another entertainment building known as a *circus*.

Circus buildings were built specifically for the purpose of chariot racing and had nothing at all to do with the modern definition of "circus." Instead these long narrow buildings were designed not only to house the thousands of spectators that would come to these popular events, but were also intentionally designed to cause spectacular crashes. For the Circus Maximus the center divider was angled, causing a bottleneck effect at the end of the track opposite the starting gate. As the incentive to win was very high for the competitors, the race became very dangerous and deadly, a detail the Roman spectators rather enjoyed.

Another unique type of theatre space that became popular for the Romans was the *amphitheatre* which is another example of *theatre in the round* where the audience surrounds the playing space. Perhaps most famous because of the well-known ruins of the Coliseum in Rome, the *amphitheatre* was a multipurpose entertainment space designed to showcase gladiatorial combats, exotic wild-animal fights, and **naumachiae**, or reenactments of sea battles.

Naumachiae (singular naumachia): From the Ancient Greek, literally means "naval combat." The first known naumachia was in fact given by Julius Caesar in Rome in 46 BC on the occasion of his quadruple triumph. He had a basin built next to the Tiber and made 2,000 combatants and 4,000 rowers, all prisoners of war, fight. Many lives were lost.

As the Roman empire expanded and battles were won, the Roman people had a desire to experience and celebrate the victories on the battlefields. *Amphitheatres* were designed with the capability to be flooded with water, allowing scale-model ships and hundreds to thousands of reenactors to replay the important moments from battles at sea. Without newspapers or television to keep them up-to-date, the Romans looked forward to these events to keep them informed. Unfortunately for many of the performers these reenactments were very realistic, and many people died while recreating the battles for entertainment.

The Romans enjoyed their diversions and entertainments to the point that some historians cite this as a contributing cause of the Fall of Rome in 476 AD. Infighting among Roman citizens over favorite gladiators, and rampant absenteeism from jobs in favor of attending events, are cited as some of the possible causes for the demise of the Empire. The collapse of the Roman civilization was so devastating to the stability of the Western world that historians refer to the following time period as the Dark Ages (the fifth through the eighth centuries AD).

The Dark Ages

During the Dark Ages, theatre did not necessarily cease being performed but the building of theatre spaces specifically to support it did cease. Instead, theatre spaces became more *environmental,* meaning that performances took place in spaces that already existed, sometimes in people's houses, in marketplaces, and in churches. It is this latter location that we must look at in some depth as history moves out of the Dark Ages and into the medieval era or Middle Ages (800–1400 AD).

The Medieval Era

One of the most defining developments of the Western World after the Fall of Rome was the rise of Christianity. For years an illegal religion, the Christian faith was able to quite literally come out of the basement with the Fall of Rome. As churches were built and congregations grew throughout the Dark and Middle Ages, the churches realized they had significant challenges ahead of them. Hundreds of years of relative social disarray meant that there had been fewer academic opportunities for the people in general and many of the laity were now illiterate meaning they could not read the Bible. Additionally, Bibles were generally not printed in the common language of the people but instead were written in Latin. Similarly, church services were often performed in Latin meaning that churchgoers also couldn't understand what was being said to them. So the Church had a significant dilemma on their hands—how do we teach our members the stories of the Bible? How do we teach them how to avoid Hell and get into Heaven? How do we do all of this when they can neither read the Bible nor understand the services? They turned to theatre for the answers.

Initially, *liturgical drama* was primarily comprised of a selection of scenes from the Bible or lives of the saints, chosen by the clergy and reenacted for their members right inside the church. They used *mansions* which were set pieces designed to look like the significant locations needed for the particular scene chosen. These mansions were arranged in the church in such a way that a series of scenes could be performed.

Two of the most common set pieces used were the Heaven and Hell mansions which were located at opposite ends of the stage and were quite convincingly decorated. It was the intent to make Heaven look as desirable a location as possible and was quite beautiful while the Hell mansion was quite the opposite. Ultimately the message they wanted to convey was that you want to go to Heaven and avoid Hell at all costs. Many of these performances were tied to significant times of the year with Easter being one of the most common.

Eventually these series, or *cycles*, of plays became so large and time- and space-consuming that they could no longer be performed inside the church. They were moved outside onto raised stages. With the move outside came opportunities for the mansions to become larger and even more elaborate. These theatre spaces were now referred to as *Hell Mouth stages* because they were now typically dominated by a large set piece representing Hell that often resembled a large fire-breathing monster.

The audiences enjoyed special effects with their entertainment and it was common to see a Hell Mouth breathing smoke and flames while screaming sinners were pulled into it or horned and tailed devils came out if it. On the opposite end of the stage was Heaven and again, all the stops were pulled out to ensure a clear message—this was a place you desired to be. The temple-like structure of the Heaven mansion was often covered in silver leaf and lit with candles to make it glow from inside. Again, the message was clear—this was a desirable place to be.

Another challenge that the Church faced was in reaching the people in the smaller villages outside of the cities. It was hard for the smaller churches to afford such elaborate performances, so instead the performances were brought to them. *Wagon stages* or *pageant wagons* were created to serve as moveable mansions.

The set locations were built atop a wheeled cart, much like a modern parade float, and were then accompanied by musicians and other performers as they travelled from one village to another. Many of the little villages had raised platforms the wagons could pull up to thus extending their playable stage space. The villagers could then gather around the wagons and view each individual scene.

Not all of the theatre that was being performed during the Middle Ages was religious in nature. Other types of entertainment were regularly offered via *wagon stages*, in banqueting halls and in marketplaces. But you'll notice that all of these locations have something in common: none of them was a permanent location built specifically for the purpose of performing theatre. After the Fall of Rome, it is not until the relative stability and prosperity of the Renaissance that we next see buildings being constructed solely for the presentation of theatrical entertainment.

The Renaissance

Renaissance literally means "rebirth." This time period began in Italy as early as the fourteenth century and lasted through the middle of the seventeenth century as ideas slowly spread throughout Europe. It was during this time period that many additional advances were made in the development of theatre spaces and the design of theatrical scenery.

With advancements in engineering and technology, one of the most significant changes to the theatre spaces was the move indoors. Now with the ability to light indoor spaces through the use of candles and oil lamps, theatre artists were free to move indoors to perform their plays. This change also meant that artists were now free to explore new possibilities with scenery because weather was no longer a concern for them.

Considered to be one of the earliest indoor theatres ever built and known as the oldest surviving Renaissance theatre, the Teatro Olimpico was built between 1580 and 1584 in Vicenza, Italy.

There was a renewed interest during this time period in the theatre of the ancient Greeks and Romans. The architect Andrea Palladio attempted to recreate indoors what he believed an outdoor Roman theatre looked like. Even the stage wall resembles a Roman *scaenae frons*. What is new here, though, is what appears in the openings in that stage wall.

One of the most significant innovations of the Renaissance was Filippo Brunelleschi's work with *perspective drawing*. This concept, which allows artists to convincingly portray distance in their work, was another instrumental development that led to the popularity of theatrical scenery. So popular was this concept, that artists even took it a step further to create *forced perspective* which allows an artist to portray even more depth in a three-dimensional work than would be there naturally. What this meant at the Teatro Olimpico was that Palladio was able to add alleys referred to as 'vistas' behind the stage wall which gave the impression of long streets lined with buildings. In fact, these alleys were quite short but the use of *forced perspective* gave the audience the illusion that entire city blocks extended into the distance. Also, the views were located in such a way that all of the audience members would be able to see down at least one of them, giving them all the same relative experience. There were disadvantages to this type of scenery however. Actors were not able to perform within the views because, only a few feet down the alley, the difference in scales would cause the actor to actually appear larger than the buildings they were standing next to. Obviously this would ruin the intended effect of the scenery. While an interesting novelty, this specific use of perspective scenery did not become widely popular.

Another artist who exploited the development of perspective drawing for use in a theatrical setting was Sebastiano Serlio (1475-1554 AD). Serlio is known for creating a type of scenery that suited all styles of plays and was transportable. Initially, he created a set of three painted backdrops, one comic, one tragic, and one pastoral (set in an outdoor location).

These backdrops could be rolled up and moved to wherever a performance might be taking place. His perspective paintings on canvas gave the audience the illusion of depth and space where there wasn't any and helped them to understand the physical location of the play.

Eventually these flat painted backdrops were made partially three-dimensional. Using techniques similar to those used by Palladio at the Teatro Olimpico, Serlio and other theatre designers began to explore how to improve upon the illusion of space in the scenery they created for theatres. Eventually the actors were able to inhabit part of the three dimensional set, further adding to the illusion created for the audience.

Another historically important building constructed during the Renaissance was the Teatro Farnese. This theatre, still standing in Parma, Italy, was completed in 1618 and is recognized as one of the earliest examples of a proscenium style theatre. The audience's desire for realistic scenery had grown after the initial developments introduced by Serlio and other theatre artists and it was only a matter of time before architects realized the advantages of presenting perspective scenery behind a proscenium frame. As the need to change scenery during the performances increased, further developments were made in an effort to make the changes happen more effectively.

One of the most significant developments, which is still in use today especially in opera and ballet, was the *wing and drop system*. This system took the ideas Serlio had developed and made them even more three-dimensional by placing some of the painted scenery on the wings that flanked the sides of the stage, and the rest on a painted backdrop which hung at the back. This opened a large playing space for the actors while still giving the illusion that they were surrounded by three-dimensional scenery.

One of the next steps in the development of realistic three-dimensional scenery was created by a designer named Giacomo Torelli. He created a new method called the *chariot and pole system*. This system consisted of drops and painted scenery wings attached through the stage floor to a wheeled wagon below the stage. The chariot and poles were then attached to a pulley system that a lone stagehand could turn. Since these mechanisms were unseen by the audience, the scenery appeared to change as if by magic. This revolutionized the possibilities of scene design and Torelli exploited this to full advantage with fantastic and beautiful designs like no one had ever seen before.

Such was the desire for elaborate scenery that playwrights began to write plays specifically designed to require the elaborate effects audiences were becoming accustomed to. In fact, sketches of some performances of the seventeenth and eighteenth centuries illustrate vividly how focus had begun to shift from well-thought-out plots and characters to extensive and impressive scenic changes. In some cases the scenery even upstaged the actors completely.

Another type of theatre that became very influential in Europe during the Renaissance were the Spanish **corrales** or courtyard theatres.

Buildings in Spain and other areas of Europe in this era typically made use of a central courtyard which gave the advantage of being able to allow more light into the rooms. This presented a very natural location for a theatre performance to occur as they not only had space to set up a raised platform at one end of the courtyard, they also had space for audience on the ground level and on the balconies above. This type of theatre was so popular, in fact, that it proved to be the inspiration for one of the single most famous theatre buildings ever built, Shakespeare's Globe Theatre.

The Globe Theatre was one of a group of playhouses known as Elizabethan public theatres. Owing a debt to the Spanish *corrales* that preceded them, the Elizabethan theatres were all built in London, England and were quite striking in appearance. Most were constructed as freestanding multisided buildings that appeared round from a distance.

The stage of an Elizabethan playhouse is dominated by the main structure known as the *tiring house* which provided not only a place for actors to enter and exit from and to put on costumes, but also provided storage as well as a roofed area housing machinery that was used to lower scenery and actors into place when needed. The flag that flew from the roof of the tiring house announced for quite some distance what style of play would be performed at that theatre that day. The Globe Theatre is also known as Shakespeare's Theatre because it is the building in which many of his plays were presented for the first time.

After civil war broke out in England in 1642, the theatres were closed and it wasn't until 1660 that theatre began to be actively presented again. By then, most of the Elizabethan theatres had been demolished or had fallen into disrepair. Additionally, the ideas and style of theatre being developed in Italy during the Renaissance had begun to make their way north. When theatres began to be built again in England in the later seventeenth century, they followed the Italianate rather than the Elizabethan style.

Once audiences and theatre artists had gotten a taste of the possibilities available with proscenium style houses and wing-and-drop perspective scenery, this style continued to develop over the next two centuries. The proscenium theatres of the seventeenth and eighteenth centuries began to make use of the pit, box, and gallery seating style which allowed audience members to sit on benches on the floor (the pit), private or semi private rooms on the second and third levels (boxes), or in seats above the boxes, high above the stage floor (the gallery).

Some of these proscenium theatres were quite ornate like Margrave's Opera House in Germany, while others such as the Chestnut Street Theatre in Philadelphia were rather plain. In any case, the proscenium-style theatre had developed a following and a tradition that has continued into the modern day. If asked to describe the layout of a typical theatre space, many audience members today would describe a proscenium theatre. This is interesting given that with 2,500 years of theatre history behind us, the proscenium theatre is relatively new.

Conclusion

Theatre spaces have changed over time, and our contemporary theatre contains many historical features. By examining the evolution of theatrical space we can identify the shifting relationships between audiences, technological advancements, acting styles, and dramatic literature. Furthermore, we are able to understand the role that theatre has played in the shaping of our civilization. Given this rich history, contemporary practitioners can make decisions about theatrical space and audience configuration to impact the audience experience.

THEATRE ORGANIZATIONS

Colleen Reilly

CHAPTER OBJECTIVES

- Distinguish between producing and presenting organizations.
- Identify the primary differences between commercial and nonprofit theatre organizations.
- Discuss the characteristics of Regional, Educational, and Community Theatre nonprofit theatres.
- Define Broadway and Off-Broadway theatre organizations.
- Identify the major labor unions that support professional theatre.

KEY TERMS

Arts administration
Broadway theatre
Nonprofit theatres
Off-Broadway theatre
Theatrical property

In this chapter the term "theatre" refers not only to the artistic activity, but also includes the organization that presents the artistic activity, and the physical building. That is, a theatre can make theatre in a theatre. Theatres exist across the United States in major urban destinations, regional centers, and local communities. Theatre in these places can be created by practitioners who are professionals, earning their livelihood from the theatrical projects. It can also be created by nonprofessional practitioners who participate in theatre projects, but do not support themselves solely through theatrical endeavors. Since theatre is a collaborative process, theatre organizations are formed to promote and sustain theatrical activity.

AMATEUR VERSUS PROFESSIONAL

For the purposes of this text, the distinction between amateur and professional practitioners is solely a matter of compensation. Professional practitioners subsist on the income generated from their participation in the theatre as artists, administrators, educators, or consultants. In some cases the term "professional" is used if the practitioner receives any compensation, even if that income does not support them completely; for our purposes we will refer to this as "semi-professional." Amateur practitioners operate on a volunteer basis. These categories do not necessarily address the quality of theatre created and presented.

Because theatre cannot exist without the simultaneous presence of a theatre space, a practitioner, a dramatic action, and an audience, there are many costs associated with producing theatre. Physical theatres must be maintained or rented. Professional practitioners must be compensated. Plays are intellectual property and must be licensed. Audiences must be reached through marketing.

Consider then the limitations of theatre revenue. Other businesses might increase the availability of the product to drive up income, but theatres are limited by fixed capacities and labor restrictions. The materials required to stage the action of a production can be expensive, and are often consumed in the course of a single production. Audiences resist exorbitant prices and most often purchase tickets to a theatre production as a one-time venture.

There are two primary business models for theatrical organizations: nonprofit and commercial. **Nonprofit theatre** is driven by an artistic vision, and sees theatre as a public service. Commercial theatre is driven by a profit motive and views theatre as a commodity of goods and services that can be exchanged with consumers. Simply put, nonprofit theatre pursues the creation of theatrical art as its main objective. Commercial theatre is driven by the potential to make money. This chapter will examine different types of theatrical organizations and the ways in which they contribute to the process of creating theatre.

Whether commercial or nonprofit, theatre organizations can also be distinguished as producing or presenting organizations. A *producing organization* creates the theatrical project and is responsible for all of the steps in the rehearsal and production process: selecting the project, casting, rehearsing, and performing. Producing organizations sometimes own or have access to their own theatre spaces, but may also rent or secure a theatre for the run of the show. *Presenting organizations* do not create the theatrical project but "book" the production to appear for their audiences. Presenting organizations often manage their own theatrical spaces, or are associated with performing arts festivals which allow for multiple booking.

At Slippery Rock University the Department of Theatre could be considered a *producing organization*. The department models the standards of a professional theatre organization in its season selection, auditions, rehearsals, and productions. Alternatively, the Kaleidoscope Arts Festival would be considered a *presenting organization* that brings performing arts events to campus by booking outside artists and supporting campus appearance by performing artists on tour. Likewise, Slippery Rock University is the *presenting organization* for the Performing Arts Series. Each of these organizations utilizes the same spaces on campus.

Nonprofit Theatres

Nonprofit theatres are organizations with special tax-exempt status. Nonprofit theatre organizations are guided by their *mission statements*. These describe the purpose, value, and activities of the organization.

Consider the mission statement of Pittsburgh's Quantum Theatre:

QUANTUM THEATRE is a kind of laboratory, an incubator for the amazing, christened in 1990, rededicated each year with the rites of spring to its mission to bring forth artists forging new theatrical ground.

They are playwrights, directors, actors, influencers. They come from Pittsburgh, from around the country, and from around the world. Productions are staged environmentally in places that aren't theatres. Quantum's artists mine all kinds of non-traditional spaces for the sensory possibilities they offer when combined with creative design. We find it meaningful to place the audience and performers together, the moving parts inside the works.

The shows run the gamut from those you thought you knew but now experience like never before, to shows that didn't exist until their elements mixed in our laboratory. Sometimes there's singing. Often a sunset. Always a reaction.

We want to move people with our experiments. We believe that the theatre has limitless ability to put people in motion. If any art can transform, open a mind, the theatre can. We are interested in real life and how it intersects with a theatrical experience—resulting in plays staged outside where a moon may rise, or not, or an urban excavation where street noises will infiltrate, or a warehouse in winter where the audience might need blankets... then watch a performer strip naked and take a shower. We're looking for truthfulness, knowing that the word is a slippery slope. We give voice to artists who invest deeply and touch the personal, even as they tell a tale, a far-off, magical, scary, too-close-to-home, knee-slapping, sob-inducing tale. (http://www.quantumtheatre.com/)

Reprinted by permission of Quantum Theater.

The purpose of a nonprofit organization must be charitable, cultural, or educational in nature. Nonprofit theatres, therefore, have mission statements that often include statements about the services that they provide to their communities.

There is a common misconception that the term "nonprofit" means that these kinds of organizations do not make any money. However, "nonprofit" or "not-for-profit" actually refers to a special tax-exempt status afforded to organizations that meet federal criteria for public service. This status is the 501(c)3 and in order to qualify for it organizations must go through a rigorous federal application process. Nonprofit organizations generate significant revenue, but in order to maintain nonprofit status any surplus must be applied towards supporting the organization's mission and not towards the compensation of individual staff or management.

There are many kinds of organizations that fall under the description of nonprofit theatres. These include regional theatres, educational theatres, and community theatres. Each one was developed to meet a specific need for its audience. *Regional theatres* create opportunities to attend professional theatre outside of major urban areas like New York City. *Educational theatres* promote participation in theatre experiences by offering performances and instruction, and are often staffed by professional theatre artists. *Community theatres* provide nonprofessionals the prospect to create theatre, and promote theatre appreciation.

REGIONAL THEATRE

Professional nonprofit theatre organizations, also called resident theatres.

EDUCATIONAL THEATRE

Professional or semi-professional nonprofit theatre companies whose primary goal is to provide theatre opportunities and education to primary, secondary, and post-secondary schools.

COMMUNITY THEATRE

Amateur or volunteer theatre organizations in residence in specific neighborhoods or regions.

Regional theatres are also often referred to as *resident theatres*. Regional theatres operate under annual *seasons*, or series of productions. Choosing these seasons is determined by a variety of factors including the availability of company artists, the need for generating ticket revenue, and the organization's mission statement. Sometimes a regional theatre is also a repertory company. A *repertory theatre* is a company comprised of the same professional artists who stage multiple plays in a given season.

Regional theatres are highly visible and lasting members of an area's cultural landscape. For example, the Pittsburgh Public Theater was established in 1974 on the city's North Side. It moved downtown to the O'Reilly Theater in 1999, and opened the new space with a production of Pittsburgh native playwright August Wilson's *King Hedley II*. The mission statement of this resident theatre is as follows:

The mission of Pittsburgh Public Theater is to provide artistically diverse theatrical experiences of the highest quality. Pittsburgh Public Theatrer also strives to serve, challenge, stimulate and entertain while operating in a fiscally responsible manner. The Public shares its resources with the community through education and outreach initiatives intended for a wide range of people with the goal of expanding and diversifying the audience while enriching the community.

Reprinted by permission of Pittsburgh Public Theater.

Educational theatre nonprofits provide theatre instruction and present theatre for schools at the primary, secondary, undergraduate, and graduate levels. They can be training grounds for emerging theatre professionals, or create more casual encounters with theatre in matinee presentations, school tours, and extracurricular courses. Most nonprofit theatre organizations have a department dedicated to outreach and education to fulfill the requirement of a nonprofit mission that provides a public service. However, educational theatres are entirely devoted to instruction about theatre or through theatre.

CREATIVE DRAMA

In the 1920s theatre practitioner Winifred Ward created a method of using theatre activities to promote learning across the elementary school curriculum. Ward developed exercises based on pantomime, dialogue, and characterization that she called "creative drama." In 1944 she launched the National Children's Theatre Conference which exists today as the American Alliance for Theatre and Education (AATE).

Community theatre nonprofits generally exist as amateur organizations. The participants in community theatres generally support themselves through otherprofessional means, and do not rely on theatrical activity to provide their income. Community theatres often operate on a volunteer basis, and are focused on providing theatre events in areas that are underserved by commercial, regional, or educational theatres.

Nonprofit theatre organizations are vital to the livelihood of theatre as an art form, and they contribute to the professionalization of theatre arts. Since 1990, the number of nonprofit theatres in the United States has doubled. These theatres are staffed by professionals in **arts administration**. Arts administration or arts management positions support the activities of the organization and align those activities with the organizational mission. Under the supervision of the nonprofit *board of directors*, or governing body, arts administrators execute the marketing, budgets, fund-raising, and programming of nonprofit organizations.

Nonprofit theatre organizations tend to divide their management functions into two positions: the *artistic director* and the *managing director*. The artistic director considers the mission of the nonprofit organization and creates the program of activities and productions to reflect it. The artistic director selects and supervises the practitioners employed or involved with the nonprofit organization: the directors, actors, and designers. The *managing director* oversees the buildings and facilities for the organization, as well as providing supervision for the administrative staff.

Commercial Organizations

Commercial organizations rely on profits from receipts and earned income. Commercial organizations are not guided by mission statements; instead they operate under the profit motive. While commercial organizations have an interest in creating artistically challenging productions, they do so with an eye to projected ticket sales, corporate sponsorship, and potential merchandising. If their proposed production does not have a "hook" for the public, it will not succeed.

When a theatrical production is mounted in a commercial environment, it is referred to as a *property*. A **theatrical property** contains the financial interests of all of the contributors to the production, and provides a model by which everyone who contributes to the production can be compensated systematically. The theatrical *producer* manages the property, including raising the funds to create the production, promoting the production, and overseeing all of the staff and administrative functions of the production.

> One of the major differences between nonprofit and commercial theatres is the life cycle of the organization. Nonprofit theatre organizations apply for a permanent status of incorporation, and only dissolve as a corporate entity under extreme circumstances. Commercial producers incorporate as an LLC (limited liability corporation) and dissolve as soon as the ability of a single production to make a profit declines. Furthermore, nonprofit theatre organizations are public corporations and must openly declare their financial statements. Commercial theatre organizations are often privatized, and their financial records are not a matter of public record.

Commercial organizations have to produce theatre in an environment that has a proven market for theatre, and appropriate venues. For this reason, New York City's Broadway district has emerged as the most significant location for commercial producing. The term "Broadway" has become synonymous with "commercial theatre," but there are some nonprofit organizations that produce there. A Broadway production is any performance that plays in a professional venue in New York City that has over 499 seats. Most of these venues, or theatres, are located in a geographical area in Manhattan referred to as the "Broadway Box." There are 40 **Broadway theatres**.

Broadway Theatres

Ambassador	**Cort**	**Longacre**	**Palace**
219 W. 49th Street	138 W. 48th Street	220 W. 48th Street	1564 Broadway
1,088 seats	1,082 seats	1,091 seats	1,740 seats
Shubert Organization	Shubert Organization	Shubert Organization	Nederlander Organization
American Airlines	**Foxwoods Theatre**	**Lunt-Fontanne**	**Richard Rodgers**
227 W. 42nd Street	213 W. 42nd Street	205 W. 46th Street	226 W. 46th St.
740 seats	1,319 seats	1,505 seats	1,319 seats
Roundabout Theatre Co.	Live Nation	Nederlander Organization	Nederlander Organization
Brooks Atkinson	**Samuel J. Friedman**	**Lyceum**	**St. James**
256 W. 47th Street	261 West 47th St.	149 W. 45th Street	246 W. 44th Street
1,069 seats	650 seats	922 seats	1,644 seats
Nederlander Organization	Manhattan Theatre Club	Shubert Organization	Jujamcyn Theatres
Ethel Barrymore	**Gershwin**	**Majestic**	**Gerald Schoenfeld**
243 W. 47th Street	222 W. 51st Street	245 W. 44th Street	236 W. 45th Street
1,058 seats	1,900 seats	1,645 seats	1,079 seats
Shubert Organization	Nederlander Organization	Shubert Organization	Shubert Organization
Vivian Beaumont	**John Golden**	**Marquis**	**Shubert**
150 W. 65th Street	252 W. 45th Street	1535 Broadway	225 W. 44th Street
1,080 seats	804 seats	1,611 seats	1,460 seats
Lincoln Center	Shubert Organization	Nederlander Organization	Shubert Organization
Belasco	**Helen Hayes**	**Minskoff**	**Neil Simon**
111 W. 44th Street	240 W. 44th Street	200 W. 45th Street	250 W. 52nd Street
1,016 seats	597 seats	1,597 seats	1,445 seats
Shubert Organization	Independent	Nederlander Organization	Nederlander Organization
Booth	**Al Hirschfeld**	**Music Box**	**Stephen Sondheim**
222 W. 45th Street	302 W. 45th Street	239 W. 45th Street	124 West 43rd Street
766 seats	1,292 seats	1,009 seats	1,055 seats
Shubert Organization	Jujamcyn Theatres	Shubert Organization	Roundabout Theatre Co.

Continued			
Broadhurst	**Imperial**	**Nederlander**	**Studio 54**
235 W. 44th Street	249 W. 45th Street	208 W. 41st Street	254 W. 54th Street
1,156 seats	1,443 seats	1,232 seats	1,015 seats
Shubert Organization	Shubert Organization	Nederlander Organization	Roundabout Theatre Co.
Broadway	**Bernard B. Jacobs**	**New Amsterdam**	**August Wilson**
1681 Broadway	242 W. 45th Street	214 W. 42nd Street	245 W. 52nd Street
1,761 seats	1,078 seats	1,800 seats	1,222 seats
Shubert Organization	Shubert Organization	Disney	Jujamcyn Theatres
Circle in the Square	**Walter Kerr**	**Eugene O'Neill**	**Winter Garden**
1633 Broadway	219 W. 48th Street	230 W. 49th Street	1634 Broadway
623 seats	949 seats	1,065 seats	1,526 seats
Independent	Jujamcyn Theatres	Jujamcyn Theatres	Shubert Organization

---

BROADWAY

Any professional or nonprofit theatre production that plays in a venue that has over 499 seats and is located in the area known as the "Broadway Box."

A Broadway production has several unique characteristics, the most significant of which is the cost. In order to mount a Broadway play a producer must raise an estimated $2 million to front the expenses incurred from the conception of the project to the opening night. Broadway musicals can require a minimum of $11 million. This does not include the weekly production costs during the run of a show which include artistic and technical staff, space and equipment rental, and union fees and dues. Producing theatre on Broadway is a high risk venture that will be discussed further in Chapter 8.

Off-Broadway productions are another example of largely commercial theatre. An Off-Broadway production is any professional commercial or nonprofit production that plays in a New York City venue of 99–499 seats. Off-Broadway productions allow commercial organizations to stage productions that are appropriate for smaller audiences at lower costs. It requires an estimated $800,000 to produce a play Off-Broadway and a meager $1.2 million to stage a musical.

Not all commercial theatre is contained in New York City, but the vast majority of for-profit enterprises are staged there. Substantial commercial theatre can also be found in Las Vegas. Outside of the United States, commercial theatre thrives in London's West End, a district similar to Broadway in the designation of theatre size and the kinds of productions staged. However, the majority of theatre produced across the United States is non-profit.

Given the primary objective of generating revenue, many commercial productions tour in addition to their run in commercial theatre districts. Touring productions allow commercial theatre organizations to maximize ticket revenue and merchandising while raising the profile of a particular production.

Wicked, a musical with music and lyrics by Stephen Schwartz and book by Winnie Holzman, is based on a 1995 novel by Gregory Maguire which is a revision of the 1900 children's story by L. Frank Baum adapted for the 1939 film, *The Wizard of Oz*. *Wicked* opened on Broadway at the Gershwin Theatre in 2003. The commercial producers included Universal Pictures, The Araca Group, John B. Platt, Marc Platt, and David Stone. *Wicked* has broken international box-office records and has played on Broadway and London's West End. The production has undertaken its second North American tour in addition to being licensed for productions in Germany, Japan, and Australia.

Theatre Unions

Commercial theatre organizations are fully unionized, and many professional nonprofit theatre organizations participate in unions or uphold union standards for contract negotiations, working conditions, and salary and wage scales. There are three main unions that act on behalf of professional theatre practitioners: the Actors' Equity Association (AEA), the Stage Directors and Choreographers Society (SDC) and the International Alliance of Theatrical Stage Employees (IATSE).

Playwrights are not associated with a union; however, they are supported by a professional organization known as The Dramatists Guild. The Dramatists Guild serves playwrights, lyricists, and composers and makes recommendations on compensation, royalties, and intellectual property. These recommendations include the right to be present throughout the casting, rehearsal, and production process.

The Actors' Equity Association (AEA) was founded in 1913 and currently represents more than 48,000 professional actors and stage managers. The Actors' Equity Association protects its members with minimum salary standards, guidelines for compensation, safety issues, insured wages, health benefits, pensions, and access to audition notices. Actors and stage managers must earn entry into the Actors' Equity Association by being hired under an Equity contract, being a member of a sister union, or completing the Equity Membership Candidate program. Once accepted into the Actors' Equity Association, members must remain current on their payment of dues and meet professional standards of conduct.

The Stage Directors and Choreographers Society (SDC) was created in 1959 and shares similar primary responsibilities with the Actors' Equity Association of contract negotiations, health benefits, pensions, and industry announcements. The Stage Directors and Choreographers Society also frequently addresses issues of intellectual property in terms of the vision of stage directors and choreographers. This protects the integrity of production concepts and choices made by professional directors and choreographers in response to particular productions, and allows directors and choreographers to protect their artistic work.

The International Alliance of Theatrical Stage Employees (IATSE) was established in 1893 and protects professionals in all theatre crafts including scenic artists, stagehands, costumers, and front-of-house workers. The union was founded largely to create collective bargaining around safety standards, but over time has broadened its focus to compensation and professionalization. The International Alliance of Theatrical Stage Employees is the largest of all professional theatre unions, and most physical theatres require members of IATSE on staff.

In addition to unions for theatre practitioners, there are collective bargaining units that negotiate contracts on behalf of producing organizations. These include the Broadway League, the League of Off-Broadway Theatres and Producers, and the League of Resident Theatres (LORT). The League of Resident Theatres negotiates on behalf of nonprofit regional theatres, and has seventy-four member theatres in twenty-nine states, including six member theatres in Pennsylvania.

Conclusion

Theatre organizations exist to support theatrical endeavors in the commercial and nonprofit sectors. There are two types of theatre organizations: producing theatres and presenting organizations. Nonprofit theatres are guided by their public service mission statements and can be either professional regional theatres, semi-professional educational theatres, or amateur community theatres. Commercial theatre organizations are driven by a profit motive and must negotiate contracts with practitioners through theatre unions.

MAKING THEATRE

Colleen Reilly

Theatre is a highly collaborative art form. The major contributors to a theatrical performance include the Director, Actors, Playwright, Producer, and Designers. Each of these roles requires creativity, persistence, and expertise.

Consider the title "practitioner." It suggests the idea of "practice." In order to be successful in the theatre you must accumulate experience in the practice of your craft. Practitioners may have very different skill sets; however, they have the need to practice their skills very much in common.

In this section we will take a closer look at theatre practitioners. Who are they? What do they do? How do they contribute to making meaning in the theatre? We will also examine how practitioners collaborate in the rehearsal process.

DIRECTORS

David Skeele and Laura Smiley

CHAPTER OBJECTIVES

- Identify the history of the modern director.
- Define "concept."
- Describe the process of casting including typecasting and nontraditional casting.
- Consider the role of the director in the making of meaning in the theatre.
- Recognize different directing approaches such as guide, coordinator, and dictator.

KEY TERMS

Antiquarianism
Casting
Conventions
Didaskalos
Realism
Spine
Typecasting

O ften, when studying the role of the director, an Introduction to Theatre student will ask, "Has there always been a director?" It's a seemingly simple question, one with an interesting answer. The modern notion of the director as a single, stand-alone theatre artist who interprets the play, coaches the actors and coordinates every design element, has been with us for fewer than 150 years (a mere heartbeat in the roughly 2,500-year history of organized theatre). However, that is not to suggest that until the late nineteenth century theatrical productions were formless free-for-alls. There has always been someone or some*thing* (I'll explain that one in a moment) guiding theatre artists as they prepare plays for performance.

In the theatre of the ancient Greeks, the playwright (who was called **didaskalos**— "the teacher") took it upon himself to convey the meaning of the play to his actors, to choreograph the movement and, presumably, to supervise the construction of masks and costumes. The medieval "pageant master" was, like the modern director, a stand-alone artist who coached his amateur actors and coordinated what were sometimes complex technical effects. The leading actors of eighteenth- and nineteenth-century productions (called "actor-managers)" were the unquestioned "bosses" of the performance process. Why then do we say that that directing is a "new" or "modern" theatre element?

DIDASKALOS

From the ancient Greek, meaning "teacher," the playwright who instructed the performers in meaning and movement and who presumably oversaw the making of masks and costumes.

The answer is that theatre in the "modern" era (coinciding with the an era usually defined as beginning in the Industrial Age in the mid-nineteenth century) is starkly different from the theatre of previous eras. In the theatre of ancient Greece or medieval France or eighteenth-century England there existed very few *options* about how theatre should be produced. In eighteenth-century England, for instance, every audience member entered the theatre knowing they would see the cast assembled into a "horseshoe" configuration on the stage, with the lead actor standing center stage (where the best light was) and the other cast members ringed around him. "Staging" consisted mostly of stepping into and out of the light cast by the central chandelier. They would expect to see actors clad in the fashions of their own time, with little or no effort spent on evoking the specifics of a different time period. Certainly there would be little question of interpretation of the pieces being presented. The actor-manager would make sure that everyone was making sense of the speeches, but there would be an assumption that the play had a single meaning that would be shared by every audience member.

These expectations—really unspoken agreements between the audience and the theatre artists—are called **conventions**, and in earlier times conventions tended to be so specific that they left little room for directorial choices. It could be said that in theatrical eras controlled by strict conventions the *culture*, more than any single person, existed as the director.

A *convention* is essentially an unspoken agreement between the performers and the audience. For instance, when a performer steps away from the performer with whom she is speaking, leans toward the audience and speaks a line in a *stage whisper*, the audience accepts that it is supposed to believe the other character cannot hear what is being said. This is a convention called an *aside*, and the audience usually agrees to accept it in an otherwise realistic play, even though it is patently unrealistic. Similarly, the audience accepts the convention of *holding for laughs*—the performers pausing while audience laughter dies down enough for their next lines to be heard—even though such pauses would not normally be taken in a real conversation.

—David Skeele

Forerunners of Modern Directors

Caroline Neuber was one of Europe's first female actor-managers. She created a theatre with her husband, actor Johann Neuber, and joined forces with Johann Gottsched who was a leading intellectual in Germany in the mid-eighteenth century. Her idea was to reform the theatre by raising production standards and improving artistic product. In imitation of French neoclassical writers she replaced older plays full of comedic stock characters, with more serious dramatic efforts. Instead of improvisation she instituted carefully rehearsed scenes. Actors were given duties like painting the set or sewing costumes in addition to playing their roles. By the end of her lifetime, this new theatre technique was copied by other companies throughout Germany.

In an effort to overcome the bad reputations that actors had, Neuber monitored their personal lives (can you imagine?)

—Laura Smiley

In England at around the same time, David Garrick is often thought of as the forerunner of the modern director. As a partner in the Drury Lane Theatre in London, Garrick, who was also the company's leading performer, was responsible for all major artistic choices. He believed in a more natural approach to acting and was quite a disciplinarian as well. He required his actors to be on time, lines memorized and "acted" not simply recited! His rehearsal periods sometimes stretched into weeks as he pushed his actors to develop their characters fully with research and preparation—quite a departure from the accepted style of the bombastic, sing-songy acting of the eighteenth century!

In the nineteenth century, however, many forces converged which challenged and broadened theatrical conventions. One was a renewed interest in history that had begun a century earlier (fueled largely by the excavations of well-preserved historical sites such as Pompeii and Herculaneum). As knowledge grew about the architecture and clothing of ancient times, so did interest in bringing historically accurate detail onto the stage. By the mid-nineteenth century, actor-managers such as Charles Kean and William Charles Macready were not only concerned keeping lesser actors out of their light, but with making sure that costume crews and scene painters were getting their historical facts right.

> This trend in theatrical production was called *antiquarianism*, and among some directors of classical texts it continues to exist today. **Antiquarianism** is a movement in the production of classic plays (usually associated with the works of Shakespeare), that attempts to create authentic historical details.
>
> —David Skeele

Creating perfectly accurate history on stage ended up being such a painstaking, time-consuming affair that it became difficult for an actor (especially one playing enormous leading roles) to manage it, and it is no accident that some of the finest antiquarian productions of the age were staged by a man who had little interest in performing himself. Georg II, the Duke of Saxe-Meiningen, considered by many to be the father of modern directing, was one of the first to take an objective step back from the performance process and concentrate solely on supervision of the production. Under his tutelage the Meiningen Players, as his company was called, were able to not only offer dazzling productions of classic plays, but also put together some of the most comprehensive historical costume and properties collections the world had ever seen.

However, it was not only the immaculate antiquarianism of the Meiningen Players' productions that distinguished them. The Duke's work also intersected with another, more significant movement that was raging throughout Europe: the movement known as **realism**. It was not merely history that people wished to see reflected more accurately, but reality.

We run the risk of getting sidetracked here (and of duplicating material covered in other chapters), but in brief, realism sprang from the sense that theatre ought to more accurately reflect the conditions people lived in. The Industrial Age saw a major economic shift from agriculture to manufacture and a rapid expansion of urban areas, and along with that shift and expansion came grinding poverty and subhuman working conditions. As pervasive as these horrible conditions were, for a long time one could find no trace of them on the stage—instead, audiences found only the usual romantic tales of heroes and kings. Some playwrights revolted and began writing plays that explored the social issues of the day, ones that took place in everyday drawing rooms and workplaces.

REALISM

In the late nineteenth century, drama began to depict characters and situations close to everyday life. Three playwrights perfected this style: Anton Chekhov of Russia, Henrik Ibsen of Norway, and August Strindberg of Sweden. It was called realism because the plays resembled situations that people could identify with and verify from their own personal experiences. This placed great demands on the actors who had to play as realistically as possible with no trace of superficiality or fakery. Konstantin Stanislavski created an acting system to attain this level of believability in acting.

Even in productions of less-realistic plays (such as those of Shakespeare), audiences were now demanding more life-like effects. Many actor-managers, caught up in their own performances and slow to react to changing conventions, continued to stage in the old manner, for instance offering *crowd scenes* that consisted of lines of extras wearing third-generation hand-me-down costumes gaping stupidly at the audience. The Duke of Saxe-Meiningen, however, was appalled by this, and introduced innovations such as making sure every character, no matter how minor, was clothed in period costume, and that every "crowd" was actually several groups, each under the supervision of an experienced actor. The effect was breathtakingly new and different for audiences, and his productions helped stoke the new hunger for realistic illusion.

It helped that he was a Duke, and could afford it.   — Laura Smiley

The new realistic work by dramatists such as Thomas Robertson in England and Henrik Ibsen in Norway represented an even bigger challenge to the old ways. Orchestrating a realistic scene in, say, a crowded family home, where audience focus had to shift between different groups of characters, was nearly impossible for someone who was simultaneously acting in a lead role.

Realism fueled the rise of the modern director, as well as other factors. The late nineteenth century and early twentieth century saw an explosion of dramatic movements that reacted against the limits of realism. There was, for instance, *expressionism*, which attempted to capture the turbulent inner state of dream and nightmare and project it onto the stage. There was *Dadaism*, which strung together nonsense words and phrases in a rebellion against the cold verbal logic that politicians used to justify bloodshed. There was *surrealism* and *symbolism* and *futurism* and almost too many other –isms to name. There was an interest in non-realistic Asian drama such as *noh* and *kabuki* and Chinese opera and some Western playwrights began combining these influences with their work.

The work of Freud and Jung gave rise to an intense interest in the unseen psychological forces that drove characters. In short, there was suddenly a multitude of ways of thinking about theatre, and the old convention that said that each play had one essential meaning no longer seemed to make much sense. In the face of so many options, the theatre began to demand not only someone who could stage plays realistically, but someone who could interpret them as well.

The range of options continues to expand today. Theatre is less guided by strict convention than at any point in history. Of course, the modern theatre is not entirely free of convention. We expect a certain consistency of style within the same production. Yet these conventions are relatively simple, unrestrictive ones (and most of us are not shocked when any of these rules is artfully broken). The modern audience, who has the entire world literally at their fingertips via the Internet, and who has seen every manner of entertainment on their television sets and computer screens, is without a doubt the most open-minded the theatre has ever known. Because of that, we are perhaps more in need of the hand of the interpreter than ever before. With so many choices to make, someone had to make choices. Thus the modern director was born.

How does one become a director? Many directors begin their careers as actors and actresses and then an opportunity presents itself and they realize that they have a penchant for working with actors, for coordinating the collaborators and for realizing a conceptual vision. Others work their way up theatre companies. Still others train via academic programs offered through universities with theatre as a liberal arts focus or through conservatories and specialized institutions. Graduate studies result in a master of fine arts in directing (MFA). Most graduate schools require some experience in directing before gaining admittance into a program. Once matriculated into a program, the directing student is able to study the many facets of theatre production. Play analysis is of the utmost importance in being able to determine the **spine** of the play. Directing methods exposes students to different styles and approaches to the work. Many programs require students to take classes in costume, set, and lighting design which help the director develop visual skills and a vocabulary necessary to communicate with the collaborators. Most MFA programs require at least a three-year commitment of study.

The Society of Stage Directors and Choreographers (SDC) is an independent national labor union that represents professional directors and choreographers who work in the theatre, and choreographers who work in the media. There are contracts for Broadway, Off- and Off-Off-Broadway, resident theatres, stock and dinner theatres, and special contracts for members working in college or university theatre programs and community theatres.

The Directing Process

When you go to see a play, the director's work is often the least obvious component. One experiences the visual components: the acting, the set, the costumes, the lights; hears the words of the playwright; listens to the sound; experiences the world of the play without the awareness that the successful, or not so successful unity of all of these components is the director's work realized. How does this all come about? In general, the director has the following responsibilities:

---

1. Selecting a script or agreeing to direct an offered script. (HINT: Only accept work that you can be passionate about!)
2. Read, read, read the play and decide on interpretation and directorial concept of the production.
3. Cast the play via auditions and/or interviews.
4. Collaborate with the costume, set, lighting, and sound designers and other theatre artists to plan and stage the production.
5. Rehearse with the actors.
6. Unify and coordinate all the production elements into a cohesive and creative performance.

When choosing a script, the director usually already has an affinity or connection with the play. Sometimes an idea or concept has been germinating in the director's mind for some time. In the university setting, there is a lot of freedom to explore. I always have plays that I would like to direct rolling around my brain. In our department, we take into consideration not only the director's desire, but the style of the play and how it fits into the season to give our students a broader experience of theatre, as well as the performance and production opportunities it provides our students.

If the play is a new work, the director will meet with the playwright several times to further develop the script before going into rehearsal. This may include discussions about the clarity of a character or the effectiveness of the scene. There is considerable give-and-take between the playwright and director and this process will continue into rehearsals with rewrites and revisions. Ideally this exchange of ideas is one of cooperation and mutual respect leading to a more cohesive script and thus a more cohesive play.

Whether the script is new or not, the next phase of the director's work is to explore and analyze the play to discover an interpretation or spine, and to create a concept or directorial vision for the production.

SPINE

Term coined by Harold Clurman in his book *On Directing* used to describe the fundamental action or conflict in a play, of which the script's plot and people are the instruments. This general action motivates the play and is one of the first steps for a director in preparing a production.

The famous director and critic Harold Clurman, who worked with the Group Theatre, says in his book *On Directing* that a director's first task is to find in the text what "motivates the play." The director must determine the "fundamental drama or conflict" of which "the script's plot and people are instruments." Called the spine or main action of the play, this is the fundamental action that drives the play.

Harold Clurman states, "Where a director has not determined a spine for his production, it will tend to be formless. Each scene follows the next without necessarily adding up to a total dramatic statement."

The next step is to determine a *directorial concept* for the production. This is the manner in which the spine is embodied within the production. This concept is derived from a vision or point of view or controlling idea that the director deems appropriate for the play. It can also be embodied by a metaphor.

Concept is probably one of the most misunderstood terms in theatre. Most of the time the word is used, it's used as criticism of a particularly bold interpretive choice: "Oh, it's *Hamlet* set during the Balkan War. I hate those *concept* productions!" Concept, however, simply refers to the particular interpretive slant a director applies to a play. The concept may be one that calls attention to itself, such as the example used above, or it might be a subtle one, such as, say, a director emphasizing what she sees as the claustrophobic feel of a play by asking for a set which seems to envelop the actors and costumes that slightly restrict their movements. Both, however, are examples of directors' concepts, and since every director approaches the play with some kind of concept, *all* productions could be said to be "concept productions."

—David Skeele

For our production of *Macbeth*, the director's metaphor was "a tornado wherein Macbeth was sucked into the vortex only to be spit out into the chaos of fate." Shakespeare's *Macbeth* can be conceived in many different ways:

Slippery Rock's Production in 2008 focused on the destiny of fate as determined by the witches. The witches were embodied as *kabuki* and *noh* stylized dancers. The world of the play was a futuristic anarchy complimented by leather and steel and techno music. Shakespeare's text was also rearranged with some lines reassigned to different characters some of whom were also blended and morphed.

Orson Welles also directed a famous stage production of *Macbeth* in 1936. Welles set the play in an African jungle and used African-American actors in all of the roles. Known as the "voodoo *Macbeth*," the production was widely praised for its innovative treatment of Shakespeare's text, and is considered a landmark in African-American theatre history.

—David Skeele

In the 1948 film, directed by and starring Orson Welles, Shakespeare's text was rearranged but all the words were Shakespeare's. He set the movie in an antiquarian style, that of an eleventh-century Scottish moor with dark eaves and caves. The witches were mysterious hags. Macbeth's blind ambition was his ultimate ruin.

In 2008, Rupert Goold's *Macbeth* was transferred from the Chichester Festival in Great Britain to the Brooklyn Academy of Music, then to Broadway and finally as a BBC film. This *Macbeth* was set starkly in the Stalin era as imagined by George Orwell in *1984*. The joyless set felt like a morgue. The witches were hollow-eyed nurses. Patrick Stewart as Macbeth created a totalitarian dictator who descended into madness because of his hyperactive imagination.

Another director might see *Macbeth* as a cowboy play, with Duncan as the sheriff and Macbeth as a deputy who wants to kill the sheriff in order to take the job himself. Lady Macbeth would be the deputy's wife who he met in the saloon. *Macbeth* could be done this way, but it might also come across as simply a gimmick—a means of calling attention to the director rather than to the script.

These are only four of the countless conceptions and interpretations of *Macbeth*. As with any play, the potential for creativity is immeasurable, and that is why every production creates its own particular world of the play, some more successfully than others, but all striving for cohesiveness and unity of elements and style.

EXTRINSIC AND INTRINSIC INTERPRETATIONS

In simplest terms, an *intrinsic* production is one in which the director attempts to conform to what they believe to be the *intent* of the playwright. An *extrinsic* interpretation, on the other hand, is one in which the director intentionally creates something that clearly was not envisioned by the playwright. Generally, intrinsic interpretations

Continued

are more likely to be found in productions of contemporary plays, while extrinsic interpretations are more often applied to classic plays.

These terms are far from clear-cut, however. As a playwright, I have sometimes had directors "see" something very clearly in one of my plays that I had never actually considered, and often I end up feeling that the unexpected choice works wonderfully onstage. Was that choice, then, an intrinsic or extrinsic one? I'm not sure. Similarly, setting *King Lear* in a sterile government building in some distant Orwellian future sounds utterly extrinsic on the face of it, doesn't it? After all, Shakespeare could not possibly have imagined such a setting when he was writing the play. But what if this production was able to illuminate questions about power and authority and corruption that Shakespeare *did* intend, perhaps more brilliantly than a traditional production? Would it still be considered entirely extrinsic?

—David Skeele

The term *casting* comes from sculpture: to cast a mold, which is precisely what the director is doing during the audition process. The director is trying to fit the actor to the role. She is looking for the right combination of personality, energy, and physical appearance that will fulfill the vision of how a character is pictured in her mind. For larger endeavors, the director often works with a casting director to assist in the auditions and/or interviews. The casting director puts out a call to agents who submit headshots, resumes, or reels for consideration. Based on the parameters given by the director, the casting director chooses those actors who are most appropriate for each role and sets up an audition with the director.

CASTING

From a term used in sculpting; to cast a mold. In theatrical terms, this is the process through which the director and/or casting director fits the actor to the role, usually completed via auditions and callbacks where actors read with other actors to determine chemistry and sense of ensemble.

Sometimes a director is familiar with the work of a particular actor because they have seen the actor's work or have worked with them before, and they will cast based on that knowledge. So, based on the audition/interview process which can include monologues, cold readings and interviews, and previous knowledge of actors' work, the director casts the play matching each actor with a particular role.

In the university setting, auditions are open to all. The director sees all interested from the university community and offers the opportunity for the actor to present a monologue or a cold reading from *sides* (short pieces of text from the play, usually monologues or short pieces of dialogue). After an evening of auditions, a callback list is posted (which usually lists which actors are called back for a particular role) and callbacks are scheduled. At this time, actors are given the opportunity to read with different combinations of actors for the director, who must decide which actors will create the most successful ensemble. It is often said that the most difficult part of a director's job is to choose the right cast. If you choose the right cast then half of your work is done. It is important for the director not only to choose the right actors for the roles, but also to create an *ensemble* whose energies are balanced and whose work ethic is focused and creative.

Typecasting happens when a director chooses actors who have a certain physical type, personality and/or appearance. In the past it was typical to be typecast into a certain mold: leading lady, ingénue, character actor. While this type of presence is necessary to make the character believable, more and more often directors seek actors who will bring originality and imagination to a role, rather than becoming entrenched in casting an actor who is a physical type. For instance, in a recent production of *The 25ᵗʰ Annual Putnam County Spelling Bee* one of the roles, a character named William Barfee was described as an overweight bully. Instead of casting an actor who fit that physical type, we cast an actor who is short and slight, but who was able to embody the characteristics of a bully in an original interpretation of the role.

TYPECASTING

When an actor is chosen for a role based on physical type, appearance or personality. For example, Sylvester Stallone is cast more successfully in roles where he plays the tough guy: the boxer, the soldier, the action hero. Johnny Depp is never typecast! He is a chameleon who has the talent to morph into any role from Captain Jack Sparrow to Willy Wonka.

Also of note is a trend in the theatre world to cast nontraditionally or color-blindly, a rethinking of casting in terms of race. This means that the director casts the best actor for the role regardless of color, and that the audience will respond to the character rather than the actor's race even when actors of different ethnicities play members of the same family. As the world becomes more diverse and socially aware, this trend will serve as a way of expressing and addressing the diversity of the U.S. population.

As the director is preparing the text and choosing the performers, she is simultaneously working with her other collaborators: the designers of the set, lights, costumes, and sound to develop the visual and aural aspects of the production. This is where directorial concept is crucial in communicating what the director envisions as the world of the play. The director and designers must work closely together to ensure that the acting style will mesh with the above elements and vice versa. While it may be easier to envision a classical play in a contemporary setting, it may not work so well the other way around. Imagine a twentieth-century contemporary piece costumed in the trappings of Shakespeare's era (Elizabethan garb). This would seem out of sync with the world of the play, wouldn't it?

Famed British director Jonathan Miller offers a fascinating idea about when it is appropriate to shift a play out of its original timeframe (and when it is not). In his view, after a certain amount of time has passed, a play enters what he calls its "after-life"—a period in which the playwright's original intentions can no longer be well understood by the present culture. The plays of Shakespeare, he argues, contain many ideas and images and feelings that we would regard as "universal," but they also contain so many Elizabethan references and reflect so much of an Elizabethan understanding of history, science, geography, etc., that a modern audience cannot possibly understand them in the same way the original audience did. Thus, Miller believes, modern directors have an obligation to explore and illuminate modern perspectives on Shakespeare's plays.

Continued

The same would not be true, however, of a play written in, say, the twentieth century. Since twenty-first-century audiences would still be able to fully understand the playwright's intentions, Miller argues that the director then has more of an obligation to honor those intentions.

—David Skeele

The rehearsal process for the play begins several weeks before the first public performance of the play. It is during this time that the director works most intensely with the actors. Each director has an individual style for working in rehearsal and varies widely in approach. There are three general approaches that have developed over the years.

On the first day of rehearsal, most directors give a speech to the company describing the play and the approach to be taken to interpret and stage the text. One type of director treats the actors and designers as "servants" to the director's concept. This is the *dictatorial* approach. Everyone is expected to deliver the look and meaning of the world of the play according to the director's vision.

German playwright, poet and novelist Johann Wolfgang von Goethe was invited in 1775 to oversee the court theatre in Weimar in Germany. At this point he was quite famous and at first didn't take his duties seriously. By the 1790s he had become a *regisseur*, or a dictatorial director. He had become enthusiastic about the theatre and had high expectations of his actors. He had lengthy rehearsal periods and expected his actors to work as an ensemble. He instituted uniform stage speech rather than a variety of dialects, and also established rules for stage movement (as well as rules for the performers' behavior in their personal lives!) He emphasized careful stage composition creating pictorial arrangements of actors on stage, and he also oversaw settings and costumes, for which he believed in historical accuracy. Our modern tradition of audience decorum can be traced back to Goethe who had rules even for the audience. Appropriate audience reactions were either applause, or no applause.

Another type of director does the opposite and acts as a creative *coordinator*, limiting his or her vision in service to the ideas, suggestions, and criticisms of the actors and designers. Perhaps neither of these approaches is ideal: one is too controlling, the other too free-form.

The third type of director functions as a *guide* or helmsman, who senses at the outset the direction that the production will take but proceeds in rehearsals and design conferences to provoke and stimulate the actors and designers. This director creates an atmosphere in which actors dig, probe, and investigate the whole fabric of the play. Rehearsals are used to search out, to listen, and to yield to suggestions. The directorial concept precedes the first day's work, but the "sense of direction" only crystallizes into a consistent stage image as the process nears an end.

To Harrow means to cultivate the soil. This is what the director does with his work. A director's vision germinates and then harrows the ground from which creativity springs forth in rehearsals and collaborations with the other theatre artists and designers.

Conclusion

While the role of the director is a relatively new development in theatre practice, the modern director makes a valuable contribution to the process of making meaning in the theatre. Building on the contributions of forerunners of the modern theatre, the director organizes the casting, rehearsal, and production process. The director also creates an interpretation and communicates a conceptual vision to other collaborators in a production.

Exercises

- Develop a production concept for the play you have selected.
- Create a one-page handout that identifies your concept.
- Select a scene to stage (two to three minutes). Block the scene in a way that expresses your interpretation.
- Select volunteers from the class (or outside of the class with approval of the course instructor) to serve as actors for the scene/monologue. You must incorporate at least one rehearsal technique into your workshop.
- Schedule a class time to workshop your scene/monologue with your actors for the class.
- You will be evaluated on your written component and the successful completion of your performance component as scheduled.

ACTORS

Laura Smiley

CHAPTER OBJECTIVES

- Identify the role of the actor in making meaning in the theatre.
- Understand the steps in the audition process.
- Distinguish between the internal and external approach to acting.
- Recognize the contribution of Konstantin Stanislavski to contemporary acting methods and understand the fundamentals of the steps in his system.
- Identify the contributions of the Group Theatre to the American Acting Method, including the techniques of Lee Strasberg and Stella Adler.

KEY TERMS

Affective memory
Cattle call
Improvisation
Monologue
Subtext

The title of a popular television show, *Whose Line Is it Anyway?*, focuses on witty and hilarious improvisational situations and showcases just one of the many skills that need to be continually developed and honed by both aspiring and seasoned actors. But to ask the question, "Whose line is it anyway?" is just the tip of the iceberg of what the actor's process entails. Frequently, my beginning acting students see a play and ask in wonder, "How do they learn all those lines?" I can guarantee that while memorization is certainly key to performing the role, there is much more to the process, and within that, there are tools utilized to develop the characters which ultimately also help the actor to learn her lines!

Those tools come into play long before an actor is actually cast in a play. Let's take some time to consider just what it takes to prepare. "Prepare for what?" you ask. The audition! The audition is the equivalent of a job interview, although the actor usually has only two to three minutes to prove that she should be considered for the callbacks. Acting is a highly competitive profession. There are many more actors and aspiring actors than roles available at every level: Broadway, regional theatres, universities, training programs, even community theatres.

To be prepared for the audition, the actor should have a portfolio of **monologues** that she can access on a moment's notice. Auditioning is a skill on its own. Auditioning can be nerve-wracking. You are putting yourself on display and are being judged on whether or not you can act! Actors love to perform in plays. I always tell my students that rather than feeling like you are being judged, think of it as an opportunity to do your one-person play! You have done the prep work just as you do for a play and this is your chance to show them what you've got!

Andy Allison in *Cabaret*, directed by Laura Smiley for the Slippery Rock University Theatre Department, 2009.

> **MONOLOGUE**
> One to three minutes of memorized text that are performed solo. Actors should have in their portfolios a selection of contrasting monologues: a comedic piece, a dramatic piece, and one or more serio-comic pieces from contemporary plays; and contrasting classical texts, at least one of which should come from the works of Shakespeare. Actors need to choose pieces that show their range and flexibility while also being age-appropriate and creative. There are monologues that should be avoided as well—pieces that are overdone, like Helena in *A Midsummer Night's Dream*. Often, actors take an auditioning class or work with a coach to help them choose monologues and prepare.

So, you have your monologues ready, what do you do next? Find auditions! Auditions are posted in various ways. In New York there is a newspaper called *Backstage* which is published every week. Actors can check the Equity call-boards and hotline, and numerous websites. For graduate programs there are the University/Resident Theatre Association's auditions (URTAs) as an option to be seen by many schools at once. In Pittsburgh notices are posted at universities, the *Pittsburgh Post Gazette* (in the Weekend section) and the *City Paper*. At universities, watch for posters and e-mail announcements. Send in a headshot (an 8x10 photo and resume), call for an appointment, show up for the **cattle call**.

> **CATTLE CALL**
> Also called an *open call audition*, this gives hundreds, sometimes thousands, of performers the opportunity to be seen for a limited number of roles, like when *American Idol* searches for contestants. If *Grease* were being cast, hundreds of young men would show up in leather jackets and ducktails. In reality, the chances of winning a major role this way are slim but there's always a success story of the director who took a chance and found a diamond in the rough.

You make the appointment and choose a monologue or two that's most fitting for the play you are auditioning for, and you audition. You have four minutes, and in those four minutes you must show your understanding of the text and character, your stage presence, and your power to reach an audience. You must jump into the role at performance energy without aid of a costume or set or other actors; your passion must shine through! And...you did it! You've been called back for another round of auditions! What happens next?

This is where it can get interesting. Callbacks happen in a myriad of ways depending on the director, the production, and the production company. Some auditions can focus on cold readings of the play about to be produced. Actually, sometimes this happens at the initial audition. If possible, I suggest to my actors that they read the play they are auditioning for. There are several reasons why this is a helpful step: to choose the monologues that are most appropriate, to have an idea of what role you may be considered for, and to be familiar with the play should a cold reading occur. A cold reading happens when the actor is given a scene from the play and has minimal time to prepare. He must read from the script with a stage manager or member of the staff, neither of whom are actors. At callbacks there may be interviews, improvisations, and several readings with other potential cast members for the director to get a sense of what you can do and how she will form an ensemble for the play. And then...you wait for the call.

BRAVO! The call has come! You are cast! You are now about to embark on the rehearsal process, an exciting time of discovery! Actors do many things to prepare for their roles. They read histories of their characters or of the time period, or both. They study real-life situations, for instance, shadowing a nurse on her rounds. Actors may immerse themselves in the circumstances of their characters' lives before trying to interpret them for the stage. Sometimes actors will transform themselves, gaining or losing weight, coloring their hair, working out intensively to achieve a new body shape, or learning new skills like playing the piano or juggling. And all this can happen before the first day of rehearsal!

What is true for all actors is that to create the character one needs to have a tremendous work ethic. First of all, you explore with the ensemble your characters and their relationships with openness and receptiveness to each other and the director. You try different staging ideas or blocking (life-like patterns of movement in most cases) which are tested and then often discarded. You discover the rhythm of a scene and the pace at which it should be played. You must be rested and prepared for each day's work. At each rehearsal you must be prepared to try new blocking and different line readings, and be willing and able to repeat a sword fight over and over to get it right or whatever it takes to make that love scene work.

Often in rehearsal there is **improvisation**, sometimes abbreviated as *improv,* a useful tool to make real imaginative situations and to make imaginative situations real.[1] Improvisation can be used as a warm-up or to explore and create backstories for the characters or to solve acting or blocking problems.

IMPROVISATION
Spontaneous invention that goes beyond the scripted material to explore aspects of character or situation.[2]

In acting classes we so often refer to what we do as our "work." And sometimes this refers to something heavy and ponderous. *Theatre Games* help us remember that a play is called just that; a play. And play is sometimes left out of our work as actors. Theatre Games help us to remember the value of spontaneity and the beauty of the unknown. They allow us to explore a situation unhampered by the demands of a script, and they can reconnect us to our fellow actors.[3]

Viola Spolin is considered the mother of improvisation. She developed her Theatre Games from Neva Boyd, who worked in Chicago with the city's poorest children at Hull House. What Boyd discovered was that when she led these children in imaginative games their spirits soared, as well as their expressive freedom. Spolin took her teachings one step further. She was familiar with Konstantin Stanislavski's system and the way it was being taught in the United States and she felt that the work was all too serious and without joy. Grown-ups now that they were "grown up" had abandoned playing! She organized a group of actors in Chicago and began "playing" with possibility. One of the actors was her son Paul Sills, who later founded the Compass Theatre which then became The Second City, the famous improv troupe. That Spolin is the mother of improvisation is no understatement!

At the beginning of this chapter I referred to the development of the character as a key component of the actor's process. Now that you have been cast, how do you develop a character? There are two distinct schools of thought: the internal and the external approach. The mind or the body. The physical or the psychological. Throughout different periods of time one or the other has prevailed. In the twentieth century, physical acting was the preferred technique of the British, while the psychological technique prevailed in America.

Internal/External Approach

If you were to approach your character from an internal perspective, you would focus on the psychological aspects of your character, identifying areas of the character's life that correspond with your own experiences of life. This internal approach is associated with the teachings of *Konstantin Stanislavski* (more on his system later!). You would draw on your reactions to situations and your personal history to inform the life of the character you are creating. Very often, actors who work this way construct an autobiography of the character, a life and backstory beyond what the playwright has given them in the text. They look for deep motivations and objectives to discover what drives their characters to do what they do in any given moment of the play. They delve into their past to create emotional responses which they then transfer to the lives of their characters. They make use of **subtext**, which is the underlying thoughts behind or between lines—thus the phrase "read between the lines." These thoughts are unspoken but can be clearly communicated by how the line is spoken, physicalized or facially expressed.

Alexis Stanford in *As You Like It*, directed by Laura Smiley for the Slippery Rock University Theatre Department, 2008.

SUBTEXT
The underlying thoughts behind or between an actor's lines.

Think for example of how many ways you might express "Gee, great haircut!" The actors explore the reasons why their characters do what they do, what influences their behavior and ask the question "What would I do if I were this character in this situation?" The physicalization of the character follows the psychological exploration and expresses the character's mental state. This is working from the inside out.

In contrast, the external or technical approach is working from the outside in; that is, working with tools outside the realm of the psychological. It uses the imagination to find a physical manifestation of the character: how she walks, talks, gestures. If you were to approach your character from an external perspective you might first analyze the language: how you speak the text, interpret a line, taste the words.

Actors who work this way access emotion through their expressive abilities rather than through an emotional response. They explore the cadence and rhythm of the words as well as the physical manifestations of the body through gesture and posture. Frequently the physical life can unleash an emotional response. Just as the psychological actor finds an external physicalization, the physical actor is also aware of the motivations and objectives, the wants and needs, of his character.

Many training programs today meld the two approaches together to create an integration of style which I believe is the most effective and affective method of creation. Depending on the role one may choose one or the other as a start-

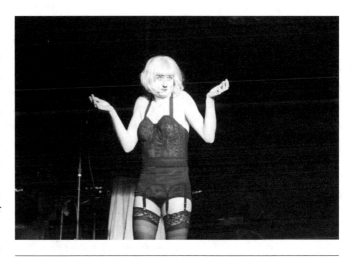

Andy Allison in *Cabaret*, directed by Laura Smiley for the Slippery Rock University Theatre Department, 2009.

ing point but in the end, there needs to be a synthesis of mind and body to create a vibrant and believable character.

In rehearsal a crucial part of the work is to discover action and reaction. In performance, this entails listening to the other actors on stage and reacting as if you were hearing these lines for the very first time. It involves creating the atmosphere and environment of the play: feeling the chill of the cold or the heat of the summer; the emptiness of a room or the feeling of a crowded room. When you act and react on stage the most important thing you create is the believability of your character in response to the other characters embodying the world of the play. This is the actor's charge to "be in the moment."

How does one "be in the moment"? By doing the things I've just described, by taking apart the text and putting it back together. Kathleen Chalfant, perhaps best known for her portrayal of Vivian Bearing, a character dying of cancer in the Pulitzer Prize-winning play *Wit* by Margaret Edson, sums it up like this: "In order to act you must take apart something that happens faster than thought, break it into component parts, and then put it back together. That's also what rehearsal is, breaking down a speech or reaction, and then getting it close to the speed at which a human being actually does it. Quite often, plays are just a little slower than life because you've added a step, the breaking down. The trick is to act as quickly as you think, which is not necessarily a function of speed. When you're doing it properly, it often feels as though you have all the time in the world. Then you can allow yourself to be entirely taken, with no conscious control. That's being in the moment, you have to have done all the work beforehand: knowing the words backwards and forwards, knowing where you're supposed to stand, and more importantly, knowing what the character is doing at every turn and why she does it."[4]

Stanislavski

The path to becoming an actor is paved in many different ways but all require the knowledge of technique and talent. *Konstantin Stanislavski* actively researched and developed the Stanislavski System in the early twentieth century. His work was ever evolving.

Stanislavski was the cofounder of the Moscow Art Theatre and the first director of Anton Chekhov's plays. In the late nineteenth century the trend in plays was called realism, that is everyday characters and situations close to real life. Stanislavski is considered the first theatre practitioner because he studied, compiled and codified a series of techniques and principles used to train actors in the creation of real believable characters on stage.

It seems a simple task; to act believably on stage, simply be natural. But Stanislavski discovered that this was not the case. It was extremely difficult to be convincing on stage. He went so far as to say that actors needed to reeducate themselves. In *An Actor Prepares* he writes, "All of our acts, even the simplest, which are so familiar to us in everyday life, become strained when we appear behind the footlights...before a public of a thousand people. That is why it is necessary to correct ourselves and learn again how to walk, sit or lie down. It is essential to reeducate ourselves to look and see, on the stage, to listen and to hear."[5] Because Stanislavski was an actor, he was directly involved in this development of a realistic approach. By studying the great actors of his day, Eleanora Duse and Tommaso Salvini among others, as well as observing himself, he was able to identify what these great actors did naturally and intuitively.

The foundation of his thinking lies in this: Stanislavski said, "The actor must first of all believe in everything that takes place on stage and most of all, he must believe what he himself is doing. And one can only believe in the truth." (*An Actor's Handbook* by Constantin Stanislavski. Routledge (2004), p. 126.) In order to quantify this foundation, Stanislavski studied how people acted in everyday situations, how their feelings and emotions were communicated and then he found ways to accomplish the same things on stage. These observations resulted in a series of exercises and techniques for the actor, which had the following broad aims:

1. To make the outward behavior of the performer—gestures, voice, and rhythm of movements—natural and convincing.
2. To have the actor or actress convey the goals and objectives—the inner needs—of a character. Even if all the physical manifestations are mastered, a performance will appear superficial and mechanical without a deep sense of conviction and belief.
3. To make the life of the character on stage not only dynamic but continuous. Some performers tend to emphasize only the high points of a part; in between the life of the character stops. In real life, however, people do not stop living.
4. To develop a strong sense of ensemble playing with other performers in a scene.[6]

Let us now explore the techniques that propel the above aims of the actor in creating a character. Following is an overview of the fruits of his labor.

Relaxation

It is impossible to tell someone to simply relax. And actually total relaxation is not the ultimate goal. What we are looking for is the release of unnecessary tension in the voice and body. This can be achieved via physical and vocal exercises. For example: stand with your feet hip width apart. Take a deep breath and roll down your spine. Shake your arms loose from your body, swinging your arms side to side like a rag doll. Slowly and with awareness, roll up the spine vertebra by vertebra, head and neck being the last to come up. With a continued sense of awareness scan through your body and tense the muscles in your feet then release them. Moving up the leg, tense your calves and release them, tense and release the thigh muscles, and slowly work up your body tensing and releasing. This is one of many exercises that are useful as a warm-up before performing on stage. Actually, once on stage one can have the awareness on mind and body while acting. Stanslavski speaks of a duality of presence on stage: there is the character and the actor.

Concentration and Observation

Stanislavski also discovered that gifted performers always appeared fully concentrated on some object, person or event while onstage. Stanislavski referred to the extent or range of concentration as the *circle of attention*. This circle of attention can be compared to a circle of light on a darkened stage. The performer should begin with the idea that it is a small tight circle including only himself or herself and perhaps one other person or one piece of furniture. When the performer has established a strong circle of attention, he or she can enlarge the circle outward to include the entire stage area. In this way performers will stop worrying about the audience and lose their self-consciousness.[7]

The Magic "If"

Stanislavski says the word "if" propels the imagination towards opening doors. It's not simply what would I do "if" I were this person. One must be more specific to avoid acting in a generalized fashion. What would I do if I were this character in this situation? Your imagination, activated by the magic "if," is what enables you to enter the imaginary given circumstances of the play without violating your sense of truth.

Deb Cohen in *As You Like It*, directed by Laura Smiley for the Slippery Rock University Theatre Department, 2008.

A simple exercise to illustrate the power of given circumstances.

A. Yes.
B. No.
A. Why?
B. Because.
A. When.
B. Soon

The given circumstances are that the characters are a mother and young son. They are in the car. The boy has to go to the bathroom.

Next try this one: The given circumstances are that the characters are a young couple. The young lady would like to get married. The gentleman is avoiding the subject.

Given Circumstances

These are the *who, what, where, when, why,* and *how* given by the playwright and further illuminated by the actor.

Actions and Objectives Onstage

The *what, why, and how* further defined. Actions are used to move a character's *objective* forward. Actions are tactics, the *how* you reach or attain an objective. An objective is what the character really wants. Acting is doing, according to Stanislavski. What you do are actions, and every action must have a purpose. This is also called the *psychophysical action*. A student at one of Stanislavski's lectures in 1917 noted the change in viewpoint from Stanislavski: "Whereas action previously had been taught as the expression of a previously-established "emotional state," it is now action itself which predominates and is the key to the psychological."[8]

Andy Allison in *Cabaret*, directed by Laura Smiley for the Slippery Rock University Theatre Department, 2009.

It is these physical actions that must be connected in concert with the circumstances to create the character's reality which is governed by the character's overall objective in the play. In the early twentieth century when Stanislavksi first started researching acting techniques, he focused on the inner aspects of training: what emotional experiences from the actor's unconscious could be remembered, mined and usedto connect and create a character's inner life. This is also called **affective memory**. Lee Strasberg, whom we will read about later, focused on this controversial technique as the basis of his Method.

Through-Line of a Role

The actor's question when analyzing a role: what does the character want above all else during the course of the play? What is the superobjective? What drives the character forward? This *superobjective* is the ultimate goal which is reached via the through-line of the character. This through-line is like a series of guideposts, that leads the character from immediate objectives to main objectives within each scene until the end of the play when the superobjective is finally realized or not. It is important to note here that not all actions and objectives carry the same weight of importance. All are not created equal! If you put too much emphasis on a minor objective or action, it will hurt the overall structure of your character. It will weaken the importance of the superobjective.

Ensemble and Communion

The definition for *ensemble* is something like this: a group of complementary parts working together as a unit. Ensemble in acting is the playing together of all the performers, how they connect and affect each other on stage, how each actor is a cog in the wheel without which the wheel wouldn't go round.

Andy Allison and Stacie O'Hara in *Cabaret*, directed by Laura Smiley for the Slippery Rock University Theatre Department, 2009.

BRESTOFF OBSERVES

This is a crucial part of Stanislavski's system. The living exchange between the characters in a scene, the communion between them is what rivets the audience's attention. The completeness of that communion helps each individual in the auditorium forget himself and enter into the drama on stage. This is another kind of communion; the audience with the characters, with the story.[8] This whole system of Stanislavski's is the most complete and practical yet devised for the training of an actor. It is designed to create that receptive shore over which inspiration can flow. It does not promise however to make you a great actor. According to Stanislavski acting cannot be taught. His method is a means not an end. It is meant to keep falseness and cliché out of the theatre. It is meant to transport the audience into the reality of the imagination; to take them out of the theatre and into the world of the characters. With the result that a mutual and beautiful communal act of the imagination takes place between the author, the actors and the audience.[10]

The American Method

Stanislavski's teachings have influenced the training of twentieth-century actors around the world. We will focus on the American Revolution of his work and the teachers who interpreted his techniques and made them their own. The Moscow Art Theatre performed in New York City in January of 1923, took the city by storm, and inspired many young actors to dedicate their training to this new kind of theatre. In May of 1930, twenty-seven actors and three others set out to rehearse in a barn in Connecticut and create Moscow Art Theatre American-style! This was the Group Theatre. Much of American training in Stanislavski's acting methods today came out of the Group experience. Innovators included Lee Strasberg, Stella Adler and Sanford Meisner, whose methodologies we will explore below.

Lee Strasberg became one of the best known acting teachers in America. He would transform the Stanislavski System to his American "Method." He explained his approach this way:

The human being who acts is the human being who lives. That is a terrifying circumstance. Essentially the actor acts a fiction, a dream; in life the stimuli to which we respond are always real. The actor must constantly respond to stimuli that are imaginary. And yet this must happen not only just as it happens in real life, but actually more fully and more expressively. Although the actor can do things in life quite easily, when he has to do the same thing on the stage under fictitious conditions he has difficulty because he is not equipped as a human being merely to playact at imitating life. He must somehow believe. He must somehow be able to convince himself of the rightness of what he is doing in order to do things fully on the stage.[11]

As referred to earlier, Stanislavski developed the technique of *emotional recall* or affective memory early in his career. Strasberg focused his teachings around this technique which at first was heralded among those at the Group Theatre and then later became the subject of great dispute amongst them. In 1947, members of the Group Theatre started the Actors Studio in New York City as a workshop where actors could work out their problems away from the pressures of commercial theatre. Strasberg, the Actor's Studio, and the Method are almost synonymously linked. And Strasberg's Method has stirred up some of the most passionate arguments about modern acting in the twentieth century. This Method is a version of Stanislavski that focuses on affective memory, or the inner workings of emotional response in order to express deep feelings when needed.

Strasberg interpreted *emotional recall* as the actor's conscious efforts to remember circumstances surrounding an emotion-filled occasion from the past in order to stimulate impulses and emotions that could be used on stage. The actor recreates in the mind's eye all of the surrounding circumstances, the sensory and emotional detail that were part of the remembered experience.[12]

It must be noted there is a difference between affective memory and emotional recall however. The basic idea of affective memory is not emotional recall but that the actor's emotion on the stage should never be real. It always should be only remembered emotion. An emotion that happens right now is out of control...Remembered emotion is something that the actor can create and repeat: without that the thing is hectic.[13]

So, if affective memory is not feeling the real emotion on the stage in the moment, how do you do that? Remember Pavlov's dogs? They were conditioned to salivate at the sound of a bell whether food was present or not. So can emotions be conditioned? By recreating the physical circumstances the sense memory of an event, the emotions can be accessed. So, the actor does not focus on feeling the emotion but on the physical surroundings of the event.

So that's great for accessing emotions, but how does that actually work in a scene? The actor finds affective memory that closely mirrors the emotion needed in a scene. He does exercises to access this emotion until he can do it in a minute with the words and actions of the scene. He doesn't use words at first, but slowly builds up the memory and adds the words in with practice. And this is where the great controversy arises.

Stanislavski realized the value of these affective memory exercises, but in later years he felt that putting too great an emphasis on feeling led the actor astray. Wasn't this like dropping out of the moment in order to do an exercise to access an emotion?

Well, it doesn't really matter if the moment being acted out is a close-up in a film. Many actors have found the greatest use of affective memory is before a camera. For take after take, this exercise can be tremendously useful. When the camera is focused mostly, or exclusively, on one actor, that one actor needn't worry about the connection with his scene partner. In such a situation, it is the believability of the emotion that is paramount. And so it is here, that affective memory really comes into its own.[14]

This is perhaps why so many Actors Studio actors are so successful on film. Famous students include Paul Newman, Robert DeNiro, and Al Pacino. However, a link often mistakenly connected lies between Strasberg, and Marlon Brando and his genius (or mumblings.) First of all, Strasberg never taught Marlon Brando.

Here is what Brando has to say about Strasberg in his 1994 autobiography: "Lee Strasberg tried to take credit for teaching me how to act. He never taught me anything…To me he was a tasteless and untalented person…I went to the Actors Studio…because of Elia Kazan…But Strasberg never taught me acting. Stella did."[15]

Yes, Stella Adler. Her work is very often contrasted with the teachings of Strasberg. Whereas Strasberg was focused on the actor's emotional life as it relates to creating feelings on stage, Adler focused on the creation of character on stage. Like Stanislavski, Adler focused on imagination, actions, and circumstances. Although she was an original member of the Group Theatre, she was ambivalent about it from the beginning and she was rather suspicious of Strasberg's technique of affective memory. As an actress she was perfectly capable of allowing the situation to carry her in the moment, and felt that delving into one's personal life for memories was invasive. In July of 1934 Adler met Konstantin Stanislavski in Paris. He was there recuperating from an illness and she had been travelling in Russia with Group leader Harold Clurman observing different theatres. When they heard Stanislavski was in Paris, they decided to visit him.

At the time, Adler was in rehearsal under Strasberg. His dictatorial style was getting under her skin and the affective memory exercises were no longer working for her at all. She lost all joy in acting. She blamed Stanislavski's system for this change…and then her world exploded!

Stanislavski said if the system made her lose all the joy she had for acting, then the system was not for her. But then he suggested that perhaps she wasn't using the system the right way. She told him of the work the Group Theatre was doing and when she talked about affective memory exercises, Stanislavski stopped her and said that he had abandoned that teaching years ago because it led to hysteria in the actors! For six weeks they worked many hours into the night. For Stella it was a revelation! She couldn't wait to share her learning with the Group!

It is important to note that an actor may be well trained, competent, and successful, but there is another key ingredient that must be present to make a performance electrifying. This is the acting that cannot be taught. It happens when a performer connects with the audience in a palpable kinesthetic manner. How to describe it? Charisma, presence, personality...it's truly difficult to describe but you know it when you see it!

Conclusion

This chapter has outlined the role of the actor in making meaning in the theatre from the audition to the rehearsal process to the performance. Much of today's acting method can be traced to the work of Russian actor Konstantin Stanislavski who developed a system of character development based on internal and external approaches. In the United States we have adapted many of Stanislavski's theories into the American Method. Lee Strasberg and Stella Adler continue to influence today's actors on stage and film.

Exercises

- Select a text with which you will work alone (monologue) or with a partner (scene).
- Create a one-page handout that identifies the objective for your character and lists three potential action verbs that you might use to achieve the objective.
- Schedule a class time to perform your **MEMORIZED** monologue or scene in class.
- You will be evaluated on your written component and the successful completion of your performance component as scheduled.

Endnotes

[1] *The Creative Spirit* by Stephanie Arnold. McGraw-Hill Higher Education, (2008), p. 143

[2] Ibid.

[3] *The Great Acting Teachers and Their Methods* by Richard Brestoff. Smith and Kraus Books,(1995), p. 146.

[4] Kathleen Chalfant quoted in Janet Sonnenberg, *The Actor Speaks*. New York: Random House, (1990), p. 252.

[5] *An Actor Prepares* by Konstantin Stanislavski. New York: Theatre Arts, (1948), p73.

[6] *The Theatre Experience*, 10th Edition by Edwin Wilson. McGraw-Hill Higher Education, (2007), pp. 129–30.

[7] *The Theatre Experience*, 10th Edition by Edwin Wilson. McGraw-Hill Higher Education, (2007), p. 130.

[8] *Stanislavski* by Jean Benedetti. New York: Routledge, (1988), p. 217.

[9] *The Great Acting Teachers and Their Methods* by Richard Brestoff. Smith and Kraus Books, (1995), p. 53.

[10] *The Great Acting Teachers and Their Methods* by Richard Brestoff. Smith and Kraus Books,(1995), p. 58.

[11] *Strasberg at the Actors Studio* by Robert Hethmon. New York: Viking Press, (1965), p. 78.

[12] *Theatre: A Way of Seeing*, 5th Edition by Milly S. Barranger. Wadsworth Thompson Learning, (2002), pp. 195–6.

[13] Quoted from Strasberg in an interview by Richard Schechner in "Working With Live Material," from the *Tulane Drama Review*, volume 9, #1, Fall, 1964, p. 132.

[14] *The Great Acting Teachers and Their Methods* by Richard Brestoff. Smith and Kraus Books, (1995), p. 114.

[15] *Songs My Mother Taught Me* by Marlon Brando. New York: Random House, (1994), p. 85.

DESIGNERS

Rebecca Morrice and Colleen Reilly

CHAPTER OBJECTIVES

- Identify the individuals who design and build for the theatre.
- Describe the responsibilities of the scene designer.
- Describe the responsibilities of the costume designer.
- Describe the responsibilities of the lighting and sound designer.
- Identify the role of the designers in making meaning in the theatre.

KEY TERMS

Costume shop
  manager
Gobo
Ground plan
'Rough' or 'thumbnail'
  sketches
Renderings
Technical director

Theatrical designers play a vital role in making meaning in the theatre. Designers create the physical reality of a production concept by creating its visual, tactile, and structural elements. Designers create the physical setting of the production and provide the things that are needed to support the action on stage. Designers work closely with the director and each other to co-ordinate the production elements. In some cases this may mean recreating the familiar, and in other cases it may mean inventing things never seen before.

The major areas of theatrical design include scenic design, costume design, lighting design, and sound design. For most productions each of these design components are assigned to a different practitioner. This is due largely to the amount of specialized knowledge needed for each of the design areas. Imagine the different expertise required to build a set or costume, and the differences in lighting and sound technology. A designer not only envisions the design but must have a plan to execute it!

Because of the many areas of expertise required to create the physical world of a theatrical production, there are multiple professional jobs in the areas of theatrical design. The Design and Process Flowchart below describes many of these including the scene designer, technical director, prop master, carpenter, scenic artist, soft goods artisan, props artisan, and props carpenter. This chapter will describe the vital contribution these practitioners make to the overall production process.

THE DESIGN AND TECHNICAL PROCESS FLOWCHART

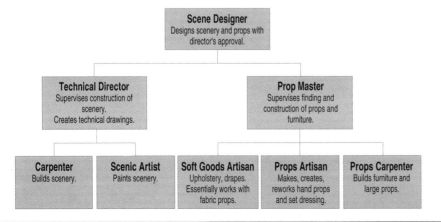

Scene Designers

The *scene designer* is responsible for creating the physical world of the play. Through the design process she must work with the director to materialize the production concept and provide the visual scheme and dimension. Factors that can influence this collaborative process include the style of the production, the orientation of the audience, and any safety considerations.

The style of the production may be the largest determining factor of the scenic design. Scene designers must be well versed in numerous theatrical styles, including historical periods, art history, and historical theatrical productions. You probably noticed that I used the word history several times in that sentence, and for good reason. The first step in much of theatrical design process is research, followed by research, and more research!

The orientation of the audience must also be considered in the design process. Different theatrical spaces (see Chapter Two) have different technical requirements and can require different visual elements. The size and scope of a scenic design is defined by the size and shape of the space in which it will be placed, and a designer must accommodate the movement (or *blocking*) of the actors without interfering with it. In fact, most designers want to create an environment that expands the opportunities for directors and actors to make spatial choices, rather than limit their movement.

One of the most exciting things about the Slippery Rock University Theatre is our ability to use a fixed proscenium space in a variety of seating configurations. Throughout our theatrical season we might use the traditional proscenium, or build thrust, arena, or alley configurations on the Miller Auditorium stage. This allows our student designers and actors the opportunity to experience their craft in a variety of theatrical spaces!

—Colleen Reilly

Safety is an important consideration in the theatre, not only for the actors but the audience as well. The scene designer and technical director communicate throughout the rehearsal process to ensure that design elements meet rigorous safety standards. This can also translate into additional training for the actors in the use of scenic elements. Anything is possible in the theatre, but safety comes first!

The process of communication between the director, scene designer, and **technical director** is supported by the use of *ground plans*, *renderings*, and *models*. These visual tools allow everyone to clearly define the plan and execution of scenic elements. They prevent miscommunication about the design which can cost the production time and resources. They also provide documentation of the production concept that can be useful for other directors, designers, and theatre scholars.

A **ground plan** is a draft of the stage drawn as if looking from above it. It allows designers and directors to communicate about the orientation of the audience as well as the placement of furniture and set pieces. The ground plan is created early in the rehearsal process, so that the director and actors can begin the process of blocking with the design in mind. The ground plan also informs the choices to be made by the lighting designer by showing the playing areas of the actors.

A *rendering* is a draft of the set from the audience's perspective. This allows the designer to communicate the visual elements of his design including the style and use of perspective. The rendering ensures that the concept of the design is aligned with the director's vision, and can also be useful to the costume designer who may choose to incorporate some of the scenic elements (color, line, and texture) in her own design.

A *model* is a three-dimensional representation of the set built to scale. While contemporary designers may create virtual models, it is important for a physical model to exist as well. This allows everyone involved in the process to see and experience how the set will operate before it is completed. The model is particularly helpful in instances when the set only becomes available late in the rehearsal process, because the other practitioners have been prepared for how the set will work in advance.

Costume Designers

The *costume designer* is the artist who is in charge of how a character looks from head to toe. This means that not only is the costume designer working on the clothing, but he also chooses hairstyles, makeup, shoes, hats, and so on. Ultimately the costume designer coordinates the entire look for each character.

The costumes a designer chooses will come from a variety of sources. Some will be found in the theatre's stock of costumes and altered or changed to work, some will be bought, some will be borrowed or rented from other theater companies, and some will be made from new materials.

The most obvious goal I have as a costume designer is to clothe the actor/character. But beyond that, how do I choose the exact items to illustrate each character for the audience?

After reading the play and discussing ideas with the director, I begin by asking one basic question. How much of the characters' personality, background or motivation do I want to reveal to the audience through the costume and how much do I want to conceal? If a character is an evil villain, does the director want the audience to know that right away? In this case, the stereotypical black cape and handlebar moustache might work. Or do we want to fool the audience for a little while and not reveal this fact until later? In that case the cape and moustache would reveal too much. Once I have that answer, I can move on to the next steps of my process.

First, I research the time period the play will be set in. While I have a good understanding of what various time periods looked like, I do not necessarily know exactly what a maid would wear on an English country estate in 1760. While we all have an idea of what the British Redcoats looked like—exactly what were the pieces of clothing they were wearing that created that look? Research is a crucial element in any costume design even if the play is set in a modern era. If I were designing a modern play that had a character who was a part of punk subculture, I would find it quite interesting and exciting to visually research what my options would be to create a believable "punk" onstage. If we were doing a modern play about the war in Afghanistan, it would be very important to me to accurately portray onstage the uniforms the soldiers wear today. Even a futuristic or "no-time, no-place" setting will require some research. In order to prepare myself for this kind of design, I will often spend hours looking at the work of some unusual and innovative designers such as Alexander McQueen.

Next, I analyze each character in the play and imagine what would be hanging in their closet if they actually had one. Some of the qualities I may be looking for and deciding whether they should factor in include the following questions.

What is this character's personality?

What is the character's age?

What is the character's social status among the other characters in the play?

How can or should my costumes help the audience to understand when and where this play is taking place?

Can the costumes help the audience to understand the various levels of relationships within the play?

What is this character's occupation?

What are the movement requirements for this character?

What Is This Character's Personality?

Everyone dresses the way they do for a reason. Someone who is a slob will have a very different wardrobe than someone who is a neat freak. Someone who is dark and gloomy will make different choices than someone who is bright and cheery. A costume designer has to be careful with this question because it is easy to do too much through the costume and forget that the actor will also be adding to the director's idea of the character. To be too stereotypical here is an easy mistake and one I am conscious to avoid unless the style of the play calls for it.

What Is the Character's Age?

High school and college theatre departments have a unique challenge on their hands in that many of the actors cast will not be the same age as the characters they are portraying. This results in the need for a lot of extra effort through costume and makeup in order to give the audience the illusion of age. In professional theatre, it is much more likely that a fifty- or sixty-year-old actor will be cast to play a character who is fifty or sixty years old. In educational theater, that is not always possible.

What Is the Character's Gender?

Interestingly enough, this comes up quite often. Not only do directors sometimes like to do what we call gender-bending, which is casting an actor to portray a member of their opposite sex, but there are many plays, both classical and modern, that require a character to portray the opposite sex at points in the play.

Twelfth Night, by William Shakespeare, is a good example of a play in which a female character, Viola, dresses as a man through much of the action of the play and then reveals herself to be a woman at the end. Given that all actors in Shakespeare's day were male, it may also be surprising to note that the original Juliet in *Romeo and Juliet* was first played by a young man.

What Is the Character's Social Status Among the Other Characters in the Play?

Within any group of characters there will be some who are of a higher social status than others. This may reflect the differences between the rich and poor characters. It may reflect differences in their power status. In any case it is often helpful to at least subtly suggest these differences to the audience.

How Can or Should My Costumes Help the Audience to Understand When and Where This Play Is Taking Place?

The costumes of a play can do a lot to set the play. Clothing looks different in different time periods. Clothing looks different from country to country. Even without a set design, the costumes can aid the audience in understanding whether we are watching a play set in the past, present, or future, and they can aid in understanding where the play is taking place. Football uniforms tell the audience we are at a football game without actually needing the football field. The bustle gown and black top hats help the audience understand that the library the actors are in is from the 1800s rather than a modern time period.

Can the Costumes Help the Audience to Understand the Various Levels of Relationships Within the Play?

This can be a particularly difficult challenge but often become necessary especially with large plays such as Shakespeare's *Romeo and Juliet* where there are two distinct feuding families and a variety of characters who belong to one family or the other. One way to help the audience keep straight who belongs to each is through the use of color. For example, I could choose from the start that anyone related to Juliet will be in shades of blue while anyone from Romeo's family will wear shades of red. This would help the audience to keep straight who belongs to which family whenever they appeared on stage.

What Is This Character's Occupation?

What people do for a living will often greatly affect what they wear. A soldier in any time period will look different than a civilian. A maid will look different than the people living in the house she cleans. A businesswoman will look different than the waitress serving her at a restaurant.

What Are the Movement Requirements for This Character?

If a character will be doing significant movement during the play such as stage combat, dancing, and falls, the costume I design must be able to move with the actor. To ask an actor to sword-fight in clothes that do not allow them to lunge and fall, is asking for a "wardrobe malfunction." There are sewing tricks that can be done to clothing, and fabrics that can be chosen, that will work to accommodate the needs of the movement but you must know this going into the process— not after the actor has split his pants trying to leap across the stage.

These are just some examples of the questions I need to answer before I can begin choosing what each garment is that the characters wear. Very often, the choices are subtle but they must be made for a reason. Remember that everything that you see on stage was chosen to be there. Nothing is arbitrary as we all began with a blank stage and a naked actor.

Color can have a very significant effect on an audience's interpretation of a character. If a character walks out in a long black dress, we might find her elegant. If the same character appeared in the same dress, but in red, we might find her more risqué or daring.

Texture can have a significant impact on our understanding as well. A suit made of rough cotton will hang stiffly and would be more appropriate for a poor character, while the same suit made out of fine silk or wool would give us the impression of someone who can afford to buy his suits from an expensive tailor.

Line can help a character look softer and possibly more feminine if curvilinear, while costumes with a lot of hard, straight lines will appear more austere and masculine.

Now that I have made these decisions, my next job is to put these ideas on paper. I need to illustrate my designs so that a director can see what is in my head and approve or, if necessary, disapprove the look for each character.

First I begin by doing some simple pencil sketches of my ideas on paper. These are called **'rough' or 'thumbnail' sketches** and are usually quick and simple.

Once the director and I are in agreement, I begin the process of creating **renderings** which are color paintings or collages representing the look for each costume within the show.

Details such as hairstyles, shoes, accessories and costume props will also be illustrated at this point because, after they are approved by the director, these renderings will then be passed on to a whole team of people in the costume shop to bring the ideas to life.

While the educational costume shop I am in charge of typically consists of myself, a part-time student assistant, and a few volunteers, professional theatre costume shops are usually made up of many people, each assigned to fulfill a specific set of tasks.

First, there is the **costume shop manager** who is in charge of managing the resources, staff, and workload of the costume shop. This person helps to decide how the costume budget should be spent and is usually quite knowledgeable about where to find items a designer needs—especially when designing for a different time period.

Next there is the *draper* who is an expert dressmaker and tailor. Not only do they have the skills to know how to make a designer's rendering come to life in fabric, they also know how to expertly fit the garments to the actors' specific measurements and they know how to do all of this for clothes from across history. They understand not only how to fit pre-made garments but they also know how to draft patterns for costumes that are to be made from scratch. There are not many people around today who understand the intricacies of an 1880s bustle gown or have a reason to know how to construct a man's Renaissance doublet, so it makes the wealth of knowledge a draper has rather remarkable.

Working closely with the *draper* is the *first hand*, who is often training to become a draper. This is the person who

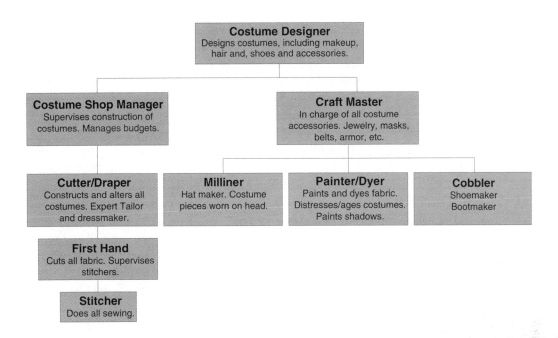

Costume Designer
Designs costumes, including makeup, hair and, shoes and accessories.

Costume Shop Manager
Supervises construction of costumes. Manages budgets.

Craft Master
In charge of all costume accessories. Jewelry, masks, belts, armor, etc.

Cutter/Draper
Constructs and alters all costumes. Expert Tailor and dressmaker.

Milliner
Hat maker. Costume pieces worn on head.

Painter/Dyer
Paints and dyes fabric. Distresses/ages costumes. Paints shadows.

Cobbler
Shoemaker Bootmaker

First Hand
Cuts all fabric. Supervises stitchers.

Stitcher
Does all sewing.

takes the draper's pattern and cuts it from the fabric the designer has chosen. While this seems simple enough, the first hand not only knows how to cut the pattern out with all of the proper allowances for the seams, she also knows how to lay it out so that patterns will match up properly and the garment will hang properly. The first hand also supervises the *stitchers*.

The *stitchers* are the team of people who take the garments the draper has marked for alterations or the fabric the first hand has cut out, and finish them. This includes not only sewing the seams of a garment but also all of the finishing work including adding zippers, buttons, decorative trims, and embroidery, and any other part of the process that involves sewing. It is quite common for each draper in a costume shop to have at least one first hand and two or three stitchers assisting them.

While we tend to think of most costumes as fabric, there are many items that an actor may be asked to wear that are not typical pieces of sewn clothing. For instance, armor, shoes, hats, jewelry, and other accessories all fall into this category. In these cases, the *craftmaster* will create or supervise other artisans in creating these items.

Working alongside the craftmaster will be the *painter/dyer* who is in charge of dyeing any fabric whose color the designer wants to change. As a designer, I don't always have a hard time finding the perfect garment or piece of fabric I want for a costume but it is rarely the exact color I want it to be. In this case, a painter/dyer has the skills and color knowledge to mix the right dyes to change it for me. Additionally, the painter/dyer will also do any distressing or aging of costumes that need to have that look. They will also sometimes paint shadows into the folds of a costume to help combat the bright stage lights that can make scenery and costumes look very flat onstage. They may paint trims, false embroidery, and other special effects onto a costume as well.

Also working with the craft master will be the *cobbler* and the *milliner*. As it is very difficult to find shoes from past time periods, and impossible to afford to purchase the real thing, the cobbler is in charge of making or altering any footwear the designer needs for a performance. Additionally since hats were a common accessory in most time periods all the way up through the 1950s, a theatre will also sometimes employ a milliner who specifically makes hats. If a theatre company specializes in producing works of classical theatre, the jobs of cobbler and milliner can easily be full-time positions.

Wigmakers and *makeup designers* will be employed when a designer needs to significantly alter the style or color of an actor's hair or needs to alter the look of their face or create other makeup special effects. While professional actors, both male and female, are usually trained to be able to do their own basic stage makeup, they are not expected to do their own prosthetics, special effects, or blood effects. As the actors are also not required to dye or cut their own hair, and hairstyles vary greatly from one time period to the next, wigmakers and stylists can very valuable to bring on board.

Finally the *wardrobe crew* is brought in. These are the people who work to maintain, clean, repair, and care for the costumes once the show has opened to audiences. They are also there to help dress the actors when the costumes are complicated or when the actor must perform a quick-change (usually defined as an actor having to change from one costume to another in a very short amount of time, often one minute or less). Depending on the longevity of the run of the play, the wardrobe crew may be employed for days or, in the case of some long-running Broadway performances, for years. Imagine the work it takes to keep the costumes looking as good at their last performance as they did at the first!

As you can see, there is a lot of thought and physical effort put into choosing the clothing the actors will wear as their characters. While many of these choices are meant to be subtle so that they will not be overly obvious to the audience and draw them out of their enjoyment of the performance, the combined effect of these efforts adds to the overall production.

Lighting Designers

Like the scenic and costume designers, the *lighting designer* makes choices that contribute to the realization of the production concept. While lighting design is a fairly recent development in theatrical practice, it is rapidly evolving as lighting technology advances. The lighting designer works very closely with the director and scene designer, and works to create lighting effects that contribute to the mood, atmosphere, and the sensory experience of the audience. Lighting design can also contribute to the audience's understanding of location and time of day.

In creating a lighting design, the lighting designer considers four dimensions of lighting: *intensity*, *color*, *pattern*, and *focus*. The *intensity* of the light is determined by the type of lighting instrument, the strength of its lamp, and the use of any filters. Like all of the lighting dimensions the lighting intensity contributes to the mood, definition of time and place, and dimension of scenic elements. The *color* of the light is determined by the use of lighting gels added to the lighting instruments. A lighting designer uses color to communicate mood and impact the atmosphere of the production. *Pattern* is defined by the type of lamp and the use of special inserts known as **gobos**. Pattern can create shapes on stage, provide texture, and give a sense of place. *Focus* refers to the orientation of the lamps, and is implemented by the lighting designer in the placement and distribution of the lighting instruments. The lighting designer creates a lighting plot to communicate their plan for hanging the lighting instruments.

GOBO

A template for a pattern inserted in a lighting instrument to create a projection or image on the stage.

Sound Designers

Sound design can have a profound impact on the mood or atmosphere of a given moment on stage. It can also provide a sense of time, place, and even memory. Like lighting design, sound design is a rapidly evolving field as technology is developed to support it. Sound designers collaborate with the director to realize a production concept by creating ambient sound, practical sound, and sound that underscores the action of the play.

Ambient sound refers to sound effects that provide information about a particular location. These sound effects are often recorded and might include wind, birds, traffic, office noise, and similar familiar noises. *Practical* sound effects refer to sound design elements that must be created live on stage. A sound design that *underscores* the action of the play resembles a traditional soundtrack, and can create a kind of commentary on the action. A sound designer often has to acquire the rights for tracks included in the underscore.

In addition to creating the sound cues, the sound designer creates a sound plot that describes the placement of microphones, speakers, and other sound auxiliary equipment. This plot must be coordinated with the set designer, lighting designer, and costume designer.

Conclusion

While this chapter has provided an overview of the responsibilities of the scene designer, costume designer, lighting designer, and sound designer, it by no means exhausts the vital role each plays in the process of making theatre. Each designer undergoes a process of research and documentation that not only communicates their vision for the design elements, but also their plan for the execution of that vision. Through drawings, plots, and renderings their unique visions emerge and remain as a record of the production. Designers bridge the gap between the imaginary and the tangible, and translate the creative vision into material reality. That is how they contribute to the making of meaning in the theatre.

Exercises

- Create a design concept for the scene or monologue selected.
- Create a one-page handout that articulates your design statement.
- **Scenic Design**: Create one of the following:
  o A ground plan and a poster-size collage of magazine clippings or photographs that reflect your scenic design.
  o A color rendering.
  o A shoebox diorama with a multidimensional realization of your design.
- **Costume Design**: Create a poster-size collage of magazine clippings or sketches that reflect your costume design.
- **Sound Design**: Create a ten- to twelve-minute soundtrack for the sound design. Your handout must include the track names and artists.
- Design projects will be displayed for the class. Presentation is optional.
- You will be evaluated on your written component and the timely submission of your design.

PLAYWRIGHTS

David Skeele

CHAPTER OBJECTIVES

- Define action as central to the creation of dramatic text and identify the differences between psychological and physical action.
- Understand the role of the playwright in making meaning in the theatre.
- Discuss different ways that playwrights are inspired to make art.
- Understand the differences between real speech and dramatic text.
- Recognize the importance of creating unique and individualized characters.

KEY TERMS

Eugene O'Neill
Gregory Kotis
Lisa Kron
Moisés Kaufman
Paula Vogel

Of all the artists who come together to create theatre, the playwright occupies a unique position. Directors begin their process with a written script (or, alternately, with a group of actors who are ready to help them create one). Actors and designers also begin with the script, along with any interpretive guidelines or inspiration provided by the director. Stage carpenters and electricians begin with plans provided by the designers. Members of the various backstage crews begin with nearly finished productions.

The playwright, on the other hand, typically begins with nothing. Every play I've ever written has begun life as a sheet of paper or a blank computer screen. How does the playwright deal with this challenge—the challenge of creating art out of thin air?

Playwriting and the Problem of Inspiration

Some playwrights find that their own lives provide rich dramatic material. **Eugene O'Neill**, considered one of the finest playwrights America ever produced, drew heavily on his own family experience to write his Pulitzer Prize-winning 1942 masterpiece *Long Day's Journey Into Night*. The story and characters mirrored those of his own painful upbringing so closely, in fact, that he never submitted the play for production in his lifetime. It was finally staged in 1956—three years after his death. Playwright/performer **Lisa Kron** has fashioned many of her plays, such as *2.5 Minute Ride* and *101 Humiliating Stories*, directly from her own experiences.

There are pitfalls to autobiographical writing, however. Young playwrights (and even experienced playwrights) often find that they have a lack of objectivity about their own lives, making it difficult for them to decide what material to include and what material to discard. Virtually everything in your own life seems meaningful and important to you, but it is not always easy to tell how much of it will translate into a meaningful and important experience for others. For instance, a violent argument you were part of may have been traumatic for you or exciting for you, but will it necessarily prove dramatic when recounted and staged for people who weren't there?

This is one reason most playwrights employ a *partially* or *indirectly* auto-biographical approach, perhaps beginning with their own experiences, but transforming the circumstances and the characters enough that they maintain some objectivity about them. (It is worth noting here that NO playwright can completely remove the element of autobiography from his writing. Playwrights are artists, which means that everything they do will be colored by their own unique upbringing and experiences—and that is exactly as it should be!)

Playwright **Paula Vogel** suffered a terrible personal tragedy, losing her brother to AIDS just before they were to embark on a European vacation. Her response was to create the play *The Baltimore Waltz*, but in it she chose not to recount directly the story of his struggle with the disease. Instead, she created a darkly comic vision of what their trip through Europe might have been, in the process changing the terminally ill character from the brother to the sister.

Similarly, **Gregory Kotis'** hit musical *Urinetown* was inspired by an experience he had in Paris, when poor budget planning forced him to spend several days rationing change to use in that city's pay bathrooms. Again, rather than telling the story of a financially strapped playwright trying to survive in Paris, he used his experience to help him create a tale of a dystopian world where all bathrooms are pay bathrooms controlled by a power-mad corporation.

Sometimes playwrights use historical events and/or present-day news stories as inspiration. Sharon Pollock researched the Lizzie Borden murder case of 1893 in order to create her chilling play *Blood Relations*. **Moisés Kaufman** and his Tectonic Theatre Company used another famous murder—the vicious attack on gay college student Matthew Shepard in Laramie, Wyoming—as the backdrop of *The Laramie Project*. In this *documentary play*, playwright Kaufman and his actors interviewed hundreds of Laramie residents, eventually assembling the interview dialogue into an acclaimed three-act play that measures the reverberations of the murder on an entire community.

Upon occasion, playwrights have successfully *combined* the historical event and the present-day news story. In the 1970s, Howard Brenton wrote a play entitled *The Romans In Britain*. Though on its surface it is an historical play about Roman oppression of the native British populace, it is a thinly disguised condemnation of then-current British policies toward Ireland. Probably the most famous example of a playwright using an historical event as an analogy for a contemporary one is Arthur Miller's play *The Crucible*. Though it seems to be an investigation of the famous Salem witch trials of the late seventeenth century, those trials were clearly intended by Miller to be a metaphor for the persecution of American citizens in the 1950s by Senator Joseph McCarthy and the House Committee on Un-American Activities (HUAC).

Some playwrights freely admit to using their own fears and anxieties and anger as inspiration, finding it therapeutic to hold them at arm's length and examine them. As someone who writes plays of supernatural horror, I'm definitely one of those playwrights. My way of beginning one of these plays is to sit in a dark room watching a horror movie or an episode of *Ghost Hunters*, trying to get in touch with the things that truly frighten me.

Many playwrights talk about a play being launched by a single visual image. Such an image might be held in the playwright's mind for months or even years before he understands what it means or realizes how he want to use it. Again, I'll use my own playwriting as an example. For years, I had an image that I simply knew would one day be part of the opening of a play: an image of a young man in a garish heavy-metal t-shirt and a leather vest, wearing an expression at once intense and vacant, sitting next to a throbbing turbine. What did it mean? Who knew? I just felt compelled by this young man and his expression of unfocused rage. When a playwriting professor suggested writing a play for "two guys and a deck of cards," everything came together: I used the image as the basis for *King of Sticks*, a play about a deluded, troubled young man who works in the basement of a paper mill and believes he has the ability to read tarot cards.

Often, plays are simply inspired by ideas for characters: characters who just appear in the playwright's mind's-eye (as in the examples above), characters based on people the playwright observes in real life or people with whom she is acquainted. How many times have you looked at your crazy roommate or eccentric uncle and said "this guy ought to be in a play" (or movie or novel)? Well, if you're a playwright, you're blessed with the ability to actually write that play!

It is fitting that we've come to the subject of character now, for no matter how or where you find inspiration to begin your play, it is character that must be your primary building-block.

Dramatic Characters

Gary Garrison, head of the playwriting program at New York University's Tisch School of the Arts, likes to begin his classes by writing a wonderfully blunt quote on the chalkboard, capitalized for emphasis: "YOUR PLAY WILL NEVER BE MORE DRAMATIC OR INTERESTING THAN THE CHARACTERS YOU PUT IN IT." It's a simple but crucial piece of advice. For many playwrights, it is the *idea* or the *theme* that provides that first spark of excitement. That of course is fine, but far too many beginning playwrights fail to understand that ideas and themes are not in and of themselves dramatic. It is not until the ideas and themes find expression in the mouths of fully realized characters that a play becomes dramatic.

So what is a fully realized character? Think about the characters who have captured your imagination and interest in plays, or in films or television shows or novels. Why did they intrigue you? Certainly it's not a simple matter of being likeable. Some of the most fascinating and memorable characters in dramatic literature have been villains such as Shakespeare's Richard III or Tony Kushner's Roy Cohn. It's been said that great stories are stories that combine the unique and the universal, and the same could be said about great characters: they are unique, different enough from us that we feel we can learn something new from them; and at the same time they are universal, containing recognizable human attributes to which we can all relate.

Of course, building these unique and relatable characters is easier said than done, or everyone would be a successful playwright. How do playwrights do it? They do it the same way anyone who is building anything does: by using tools. And, I would argue, the single most important tool a playwright can bring to bear on the problem of creating memorable characters is empathy. The playwright is an artist who has much in common with the actor. Like the actor, the playwright must find a way to inhabit the character, to get under the skin of the character, to be able to see and hear and feel from the character's perspective. (A notable difference is that while the actor is usually responsible for one character, the playwright must achieve this close connection with all of the play's characters.)

Suppose that a playwright conceives the idea for a play about a woman who realizes that the child upon whom she's lavished attention is a failure as a person, and that the child she's virtually ignored for years has blossomed into someone remarkable. At some point in the play, the woman, Charlene, addresses the disappointing child, Teddy:

> **CHARLENE**
> I can't believe I've lavished all this attention on you, and now you're a lazy slob who can't bring himself to even look for a job, much less move out of my house. Bridget, on the other hand, has really made something of herself. She's a major figure in an important publishing house, making enough money that she's just bought a nice place in the suburbs and an expensive sports car. I've given you everything, made every sacrifice for you, but now I am overcome with guilt and anxiety, and I can't help wondering if it was my influence that made you what you are, and if Bridget became a success *because* I never gave her the time of day.

This, of course, is absolutely wretched writing, and it is wretched for so many reasons that we may be able to come back to it time and time again to find examples of what not to do as a playwright. But the major reason for the wretchedness is that this imaginary playwright has never bothered to put himself in Charlene's shoes. She is not truly a character because he has never really moved past the idea of Charlene. If our playwright had taken the time to truly imagine what Charlene's anguish is like for her, and to fully explore the ambiguous feelings she has for her children, her monologue might have sounded like genuine human speech. Because Charlene remains an idea, however, her words sound far more like a passage lifted from a textbook.

The playwright must know not only what a character expresses, but also how the particular character expresses it, which brings us to another important playwriting tool: an ear for dialogue.

Dramatic Dialogue

There is a misconception, shared by a surprising number of people, that the objective of playwriting is to create dialogue that closely mimics the way people talk in real life. A playwright, according to this theory, is essentially a human tape recorder, whose job it is to transcribe the genuine conversation of the street onto the stage. However, all it takes to utterly disprove this notion is the use of an actual tape recorder. Record a conversation between people and you may indeed occasionally hear a fascinating word choice, or sometimes pick up on the musicality of a well-turned phrase. But these nuggets of worthwhile dialogue will be buried under a mountain of stammering, of repetition, of throwaway lines and meaningless words. In short, normal conversation, like commercial breakfast cereal, is ninety-five percent filler. The playwright's job is not to transcribe but to carefully weed out the filler, and then to shape and mold and craft until they have boiled down the ordinary into its marvelous essence. This final product will bear the same resemblance to ordinary speech that a finely wrought metal sculpture bears to lumps of iron ore buried in a hillside.

The comparison between the playwright and the sculptor is a useful one, but perhaps the stone or wood sculptor makes for an even more apt analogy, since paring away words is as big a part of the playwright's job as creating them.

For an example, let's return to Charlene's speech above. We've agreed (I hope) that it sounds woodenly, painfully unrealistic—more like an essay than a person. I'll argue that one of the reasons for this is that, like the writer of a bad textbook, Charlene uses too many words. She baldly states things when a mere hint would suffice. She tediously explains points that we presumably already understand. She describes emotional states that should be readily apparent to everyone watching her. All of this overwriting has the effect of making us feel that the playwright is talking down to us—that he or she thinks that we are too stupid to figure anything out for ourselves.

So how do we boil this speech down to its essence? What do we chip out to reveal the life hidden within it? One of the oldest pieces of advice given to playwrights (and screenwriters and fiction writers) is "show, don't tell." What does this mean? Essentially it means that audiences (and readers) would much rather decipher truths about the characters by witnessing their behavior, rather than by simply trusting their words. If you were, say, at a party, which of these people would you find more convincing: someone who walks up to you and announces "I'm very charismatic," or someone who enters a room with a confidence and energy that draws the attention of everyone there?

Rather than having Charlene announce the facts about Teddy (which have probably been at least somewhat established by this point in the play), why not show us Teddy's flaws in action? And why have Charlene state that she is "overcome with guilt and anxiety?" Can't we see that in everything she says and does? Is all the specific information about Bridget really necessary? Taking all of these questions into account, let's go Michelangelo on this stupid monologue and see if we can't improve it.

(Lights up on Teddy, sitting on a couch with a television remote in his hand. He stares blankly at an invisible television screen, every once in while lazily thumbing the channel button. Charlene enters. She stays in the doorway watching him for a few moments, anguish in her features. Though he registers her presence, he doesn't acknowledge her. After an internal struggle, she speaks.)

CHARLENE
Any calls?

TEDDY
Uh-uh.

Continued

CHARLENE
I thought there might be news from one of the…you know…job interviews.

TEDDY
There wasn't.
(He continues to flip channels, not looking at her.)

CHARLENE
Bridget called. She bought a house. In *Sewickley.*
(Perhaps Teddy grunts something noncommittal.)
And she did it all by herself. No help from me. Never any help from me. I mean…isn't that *nice?* To be able to buy a house? To just have the money to…to…
(Teddy flips another channel. In a sudden rage, Charlene rips the remote from his hand and smashes it on the floor. Teddy stares dumbly at her.)
I've given you everything, everything I could. Guided you. Held your little hand every step of your life and…look at you! Just look at you!
(Pause. A bitter realization.)
It's me, isn't it? It must be. What if I'd just left you alone? Ignored you. The way I did with…Bridget.
(In tears, she runs from the room, leaving Teddy gaping after her.)

Okay, there's still nothing here to make me devoutly wish this play really existed, but most would agree that this piece is a lot more dramatic and interesting than the original. And I have to admit that I did more than merely cut away a lot of Charlene's words—I added in a number of stage directions and threw in the character of Teddy while I was at it. The "addition by subtraction," however, is in my opinion one of the most significant improvements, since it allows you as the audience member or reader the fun of filling in some of the blanks yourself.

Notice, too, that Charlene no longer speaks in formal, neutral, "textbook" sentences. Her speech is timid, halting, full of ellipses (the ...s), and so we know immediately that she is unsure of herself and nervous about confronting her spoiled son. Teddy's manner of speaking tells us something about him, too—namely that he is so lazy that he uses the absolute minimum number of words necessary to communicate.

Action—The Lifeblood of a Play

You may have noticed one other thing that makes the second version of our hypothetical scene more satisfying: it contains *action*. In the first, Charlene is simply

We talked about objective and actions in the previous chapter: this is what drives the character to get what he wants: he does this by pursuing actions. What do you do to get what you want? What tactics to you play? What does Charlene want from Teddy? Let's keep it simple: she wants him to get a job. How does she try to make that point in the scene? She hints, she cajoles, she paints the picture of her daughter's success, she explodes, she plays the martyr.

—Laura Smiley

reciting a list of facts, which is about as interesting for an audience as watching kumquats ripen. In the second, however, she is actually doing something.

We witness her trying to summon up the nerve to confront her son, first trying to prod his conscience with gentle hints, and then finally erupting and proceeding to berate him. Even the dumbstruck Teddy has a modicum of action, in that he's struggling to get his mind around the shocking things his mother is saying to him. Do you see the difference?

Action is really what we come to the theatre to see. Even more than brilliant dialogue or beautiful costumes or dazzling stage effects, it's the promise of action that lures us out of the comfort and convenience of home, that convinces us to sacrifice our hard-earned money and leisure time. It may not be the action of film, with its realistic car chases and helicopter explosions—it is usually psychological action—but nevertheless, if a play contains strong dramatic action it will probably be riveting, and if it does not it certain to be deadly dull. We want to see people who need things, and then we want to see them fighting for those things. We want to see them scratching and clawing and seducing and praying and lying and fearing and daring and resisting and submitting. In short, we want to see verbs, lots of verbs, and at the end of the day it is the playwright's job to give them to us. (Directors and actors spend countless hours trying to find the most exciting verbs to play in each scene, but all of their efforts will be in vain if the playwright hasn't given them exciting action to begin with!)

Again, some young playwrights may be misled into static, passive writing by following the misguided notion that theatre is a "reflection of life." Life, like bad dialogue, contains a lot of filler—long stretches of inactivity, of tedium and monotony. But theatre is not really a reflection of life. It is instead, as Alfred Hitchcock famously said, "life without the boring parts."

Writers are often told to "write what they know," so many beginning playwrights try to dramatize safe, familiar situations from their own lives. Being a teacher of college-age students, I can't tell you how many idle dorm-room conversations I've had presented to me as plays. But these conversations, featuring no strong character need (beyond the desire to gossip about what girl or guy is the hottest) or action (beyond mere chattering), are usually not even slightly dramatic, and so no matter how amusing they might seem, they would paralyze an audience with boredom if they were ever produced.

Successful, dramatic, active plays feature characters faced with some kind of crisis, a crisis that requires the characters to do something: to defeat an adversary, to acquire money or position, to convince the crotchety parents to let him marry their daughter, etc., etc. In *Hamlet*, the title character is thrown into crisis when the ghost of his father appears and demands that he avenge his murder. In *A Streetcar Named Desire*, the fading Southern belle Blanche Dubois is thrown into crisis when scandal (and miserable financial straits) forces her to take refuge in a tenement apartment with her sister and brutal, loudmouthed brother-in-law. In both cases, the character has no choice but to take action to try and rectify the situation, and in both cases the odds are sharply stacked against them.

This last point is crucial, because the more difficult the objective for the character, the greater the conflict, and thus the greater the dramatic tension. Blanche is so emotionally fragile, and she is so disliked by the boorish Stanley Kowalski, that it takes everything she has just to survive, and that's exactly what makes watching her so compelling. If Blanche had immediately adapted to her new surroundings and made fast friends with Stanley not only would there be no tension, there would be no play. Similarly, if our hypothetical play is to be any good, Charlene will face serious conflict. Teddy won't immediately run after his mother, vowing to become a company CEO by sundown. instead he'll engage in some crafty passive-aggressive strategy to continue getting her financial support. Bridget won't immediately become her mother's best friend. she'll be antagonistic, and force Charlene to try to break through walls forged of years of resentment.

If we can define a play as a character's struggle, we could just as accurately define it as a character's journey, and like any journey, it must end somewhere different than it begins. Charlene seems to have begun this play as a well-meaning person who is also a woefully blind and misguided mother, doting on her son and disconnected from her daughter. She is also fearful and non-confrontational. What lies at the end of her journey? Maybe she grows as a result of her terrible mistake: she finally establishes the relationship she always should have had with her daughter, and finds the strength to force her needy, manipulative son out of the nest and into the world. Or maybe she is brutally rejected by Bridget and tries to come back to Teddy, who now rejects her too, until she ends the play as a suicidal alcoholic. Who knows? The point is that Charlene and her world must change. It may be the promise of action that draws the audience member into their theatre seat—but it's the promise of transformation that keeps them there until the lights come down.

Setting

While we've radically improved our play by empathizing with the character, listening to how she might actually talk, and adding the element of action to her situation, there is one element that remains kind of unexciting: the setting. In creating this scene, I did what I constantly caution my students not to do—I just threw my characters into a standard living room. Living rooms, like bus stops, park benches and the infamous dorm room, are what we call a "default setting," a place where playwrights stash their characters just to save themselves the trouble of imagining anything more unusual.

Can effective plays be set in these places? Of course. Edward Albee wrote a brilliant park bench play called *Zoo Story*. William Inge's *Bus Stop* couldn't possibly be set anywhere else. The living room is the heart of the American family home (many would argue for the kitchen), so naturally many family dramas are going to take place there. But I ask my student playwrights to challenge themselves with this question: are any of these settings really the most interesting you can find for your play, or are they just the first you thought of?

I suppose I put Charlene and Teddy in a living room so that Teddy could be watching television. I considered mindless channel-surfing to be the ultimate emblem of laziness, but it's possible that that assumption is also a kind of default. If I had set the piece instead at, say, the Boston Aquarium, it would have opened up all kinds of new possibilities. Perhaps instead of channel-surfing, Teddy spends each day sitting and watching fish. Why? I have no idea, but I could have a lot of fun finding out, and already a fish-watching Teddy seems far more intriguing than a monosyllabic couch potato. He's a character with secrets and issues of his own. The Boston setting requires a colorful accent and vibrant rhythms and (for me) unusual word choices. Research about the area, and perhaps about the varieties of marine life found in an aquarium, would most likely be required (and research is a good thing—it gives you all kinds of new ideas to use!). Finally, putting them in an aquarium means that Charlene didn't just happen upon Teddy—she had to put on a coat, get into a taxi and cross town to talk to him, and that raises the stakes of the confrontation for both of them. See? All of these wonderful new possibilities, and all we had to do was get them out of their generic living room.

It wouldn't have taken such a major shift in setting to change the play. Simply changing the time to 3:30 in the morning or imagining the blizzard of the decade howling outside would have also opened up new options for the playwright. The important thing is that the playwright be specific about these things. The same way playwrights must learn to live and breathe their characters, they must learn to fully imagine their settings. If the setting is chosen well and imagined fully, then it almost becomes another character in the play, influencing the action and affecting all of the other characters. (As someone who writes plays about haunted houses, I am perhaps especially attuned to this idea!)

A Final Word

As this discussion of playwriting basics comes to a close, let's return for a moment to the question of inspiration. I've intentionally left out, until now, the thing that might serve as the best inspiration for writing: writing itself. If you think you'd like to try writing a play, don't think for a moment that you need to have the entire thing conceived from lights up to lights down. All you need is the briefest opening: a bit of dialogue, an image, a character. Write that, and I can practically guarantee you that as you are writing that another line will occur to you, and then another image, and maybe a new character will enter and you can hear exactly what they're saying as they enter. Before you know it you'll have a scene, and by the time you've finished that scene you'll have an idea for the next one, and by the time you finish...you get the idea. The point is: write!

Conclusion

The task of the playwright is to create art out of thin air. Beginning with a blank page, the playwright uses setting, action, and character to create the script that guides the directors, actors, and designers towards production. While the playwright is often an invisible collaborator, they are central to the process of making meaning in the theatre.

Exercises

Writing from a Premise

Sometimes it is easier to conceive of a story when you have a sense of what you want to "prove."

Following is a list of well-known proverbs. Choose one that you find especially interesting or provocative and jot down a brief summary of a story that might demonstrate the truth of the proverb. (Alternately, you might have fun creating a story that demonstrates the *un*truth of the proverb!)

- A little knowledge is a dangerous thing.
- A friend to all is a friend to none.
- A man's got to do what a man's got to do.
- A rolling stone gathers no moss.
- Act in haste, repent at leisure.
- Actions speak louder than words.
- Any port in a storm.
- Ashes of love are cold as ice.
- Bend like a willow or break like an oak.

Creating Interesting Dialogue

One of the biggest mistakes young playwrights often make is creating characters who all sound the same.

As a playwright, you have a nearly infinite variety of verbal expression to draw from! Don't settle for cliché or characters who sound like they're reading from textbooks.

The following are a list of "dialogue attributes." Pick two that sound interesting to you (make sure they differ from *each other*!), and use them to create a short dialogue between two characters.

Don't worry about plot for now. Just have fun letting two people with wildly different communication methods talk to each other!

12 Dialogue Attributes:
1. Gruff; economical with words.
2. Sinuous; smooth; snake-like with words.
3. Uneducated, and overcompensating through use of words.
4. Barely able to find the breath to convey all the words in his or her head.
5. Lyrical; a poet.
6. Always groping for words; rarely finding them.
7. Everything expressed in a nervous laugh.
8. Sensualist; chews and savors words.
9. Speaks words as though she or he hates the taste of them.
10. Uses sounds of words to seduce.
11. Uses sounds of words to hurt or seize power.
12. Very educated; tries to hide it through use of words.

Character Objectives

Remember, drama is driven by the needs of the characters. Write a short play using the following template:

Two characters, **A** and **B**, who know each other.

Setting is someplace interesting.

A is in crisis, and comes to **B** with a desperate need. **B** is shocked by the need. **A** makes several attempts to get **B** to go along with him/her, but **B** resists. Finally, **B** reveals his/her own need, which shocks **A** even more. At the end, the relationship is either strengthened or shattered or in some way seriously altered.

PRODUCERS

Colleen Reilly

CHAPTER OBJECTIVES

- Understand the role of producers in making meaning in the theatre.
- Understand the responsibilities of the producer in the commercial theatre.
- Identify the process of producing commercial theatre.
- Understand the responsibilities of the managing director in the nonprofit theatre.
- Understand the challenges of producing theatre in the current economic climate.

KEY TERMS

Cost disease
Dramaturg
Property
Run
Royalty pool

I think the best place to start a discussion of producers is with the Broadway musical of the same name. *The Producers*, a musical written by Mel Brooks and Thomas Meehan, opened on Broadway in 2001 and tells the story of a down-on-his-luck Broadway producer who schemes to make a profit by staging the worst musical ever. Set in New York in 1957, the premise of the musical rests on the idea that if a surplus of money is raised to invest in a production that no one has any interest in salvaging, the producers can pocket the money for personal gain. They choose a property called *Springtime for Hitler*, and hire an incompetent director along with an unknown lead actress. Unfortunately, the intent of staging a ridiculous production backfires and they find themselves with a hit on their hands.

The musical raises some interesting questions about the strange economy of producing commercial theatre, and the ethics of the person responsible for the financial matters surrounding the production. Max Bialystock, the fictional producer in *The Producers* is based on a romanticized notion of commercial production from the heyday of Broadway in the 1950s. This chapter will explore the reality of producing theatre in our current economic climate.

Some critics see Max Bialystock as a comic representation of Broadway producer David Merrick. David Merrick was an award winning producer on Broadway from 1954 through 1996. He was a prolific producer responsible for productions like *Oliver!*, *Hello, Dolly!*, and *42ⁿᵈ Street*. He was (in)famous for his publicity stunts which included finding New Yorkers who shared the names of leading theatre critics, soliciting their approval of particular productions, and publishing the statements in the press. In 1998 he established the David Merrick Arts Foundation to support the development of American musicals. When his obituary appeared in the *New York Times* in 2000 it read, "The Showman who Ruled Broadway."

Responsibilities of the Producer

In commercial theatre the role of the producer is a clearly defined, professional-ized position. The producer must complete a sequence of tasks from scouting the **property**, to arranging auditions, rehearsals, and performances, to managing the production during its **run**.

PROPERTY

In theatrical terms, the full scale production including the book (or play), design, directorial choices, blocking and acting choices. The term *property* allows a producer to treat the dynamic creative processes contributing to a theatri-cal creation as a single financed outcome; the product of the collaborative rehearsal process in theatre becomes a single property for the producer that can define the distribution of revenue and expenses.

RUN

The sequence of performances of a single theatrical property. In the commercial sector the *run* of the show is determined by its financial viability. In the nonprofit sector, the run of the show is normally predetermined by the season schedule in a fixed term.

The producer serves the financial interests of the production, but this does not necessarily mean that he is out of touch with the artistic goals of the production staff. A successful producer possesses the same passion for theatrical practice as other practitioners such as the director, actors, and designers; however, the producer has the additional responsibility of translating that vision into a marketable commodity. The expertise and creativity that a producer brings to the process of making meaning in the theatre is not only the ability to reach an audience, but also the ability to maximize the income of a property while minimizing its expenses.

The first step in the producing process is to find and develop a property. In the commercial sector this often occurs as a result of pursuing contacts in literary management and capitalizing on a strong network of theatre contacts. In other words, it boils down to a "who you know" context. This is not to say that commercial producing is always driven by celebrity or wealth; often the "who you know" is determined by serious academic programs like the repertory theatres developed by universities such as Harvard, Yale, and Northwestern. These strong academic programs develop playwrights and practitioners who need an opportu-nity to embrace the commercial theatre. The contemporary American producer often creates a bridge between regional dramaturgs and professional companies for these up and coming voices.

DRAMATURG

A professional position in a theatre company that deals primarily with the development of plays. Dramaturgs support the creation of new plays, contemporary treatments of classic plays, and historical interpretations of plays. In the United States the title dramaturg is interchangeable with literary manager.

Once the property has been determined, the producer must obtain the rights for the production. This is often a complicated process and requires a savvy knowledge of intellectual property and copyright laws. For a classic or historical play, the producer must determine the eligibility of the text for public domain. For more recent plays, the producer must negotiate with the estate of the playwright. For new works, the producer must negotiate a contract with the playwright themselves. Acquiring the rights for production is often the largest obstacle to producing a play or musical; often the rights are simply too expensive to create a viable property.

Consider this: If the capacity of a theatre is 300 seats and the price of student admission is set at $5, this yields a maximum of $1,500 for a full house of student admissions. Therefore, any rights negotiated for a production in this space must cost less than $1,500 per performance in order to begin to generate an income for the production and support future projects. In general, considerations are given for the capacity of the theatre and its commercial or nonprofit status; however, you can see where the tension between the cost of rights to a play and the ability to make a profit starts!

Once the rights have been acquired the commercial producer must legally form the property. This usually occurs as the creation of an **LLC**, or limited liability corporation. An LLC allows multiple investors to create a corporate entity while protecting their overall assets. The executors of an LLC are only responsible for their initial investment, and in the event that the property fails, the rest of their assets remain safe.

In 2010 an LLC was formed with the intention of creating a revival of the musical *Godspell* for Broadway. The interesting approach of this LLC was that it was subject to crowd funding. Investments were divided into $100 units, with a minimum investment of $1,000. This allowed anyone with an interest in producing on Broadway and/or fans of the musical (and $1,000 in disposable income) the opportunity to participate in a situation that had otherwise been closed to them.

When the corporate producing entity is in place the producer next has the responsibility of raising the money for production of the property. This generally involves enlisting other investors to join the LLC, but sometimes leads to finding corporate sponsors as well. Broadway musicals generally require between $10 and $20 million in capital to produce. Broadway plays average about $2 million in capital. The capital is the target amount to be raised to bring a property from its inception to opening night.

Once the money has been raised and significant interest in the property has been expressed, the producer must secure the theatre in which the production will have its run. This decision is determined by the physical theatre's capacity, location, and availability. Producers often create longstanding relationships with Broadway theatres in order to create the leverage that they need to secure the space for the property. As discussed in Chapter Three, the number of Broadway theatres is limited by geographical location and capacity, making the securing of a commercial space a highly competitive task.

The producer also secures contracts with the artistic and production staff through negotiations with professional organizations and unions. Part of the contract negotiations is determining the **royalty pool**, or percentage of receipts that the major practitioners should share. The royalty-pool system is based on the idea that the major parties invested in the property—producers, director, author, and theatre—should recoup some income any week that the production runs. It is an alternative to the system that allows payment to these entities and individuals only after the initial investors have been repaid. The royalty pool allows the major contributors to any property to receive consistent income.

While the creative team develops the property in rehearsal, the producer supervises the marketing campaign and ticket revenues. Finally, the producer manages the production after its opens including monitoring budgets and merchandising, and managing personnel. In return the commercial producer generally receives two percent of the gross receipts. For a Broadway play this can mean as little as $5,000 per week and in some cases as much as $335,000 per week for a Broadway musical.

Responsibilities of a Managing Director

In the nonprofit sector, the managing director of a theatre often takes on the responsibilities of the producer. In this scenario the primary difference between a producer and a managing director is that the producer is working towards their own personal gain, and the managing director is supporting the mission of the nonprofit organization. This means that the revenue generated by a property in the nonprofit sector must be reallocated to the activities of the organization. Both the producer and the managing director share profit as their primary goal, but the distribution of that income is very different.

Like the commercial producer, the managing director of a nonprofit theatre develops properties, acquires the rights, negotiates contracts, and raises capital. However, a managing director operates within a strategic plan or long term vision for a theatre organization. Rather than working independently, a managing director collaborates with other leadership in the nonprofit organization like the artistic director or the Board of Directors.

Nonprofit organizations are not one size fits all, and the structure of the organization's leadership is often determined by the mission of the organization. For example, an organization with a strong educational mission might operate with an artistic director and director of education, and they might share responsibilities that would otherwise fall under the title of the managing director. The bottom line is that in creating a theatrical production someone has to be responsible for coordinating the spaces, the practitioners, and the action.

Unlike the commercial producer, the managing director does not think in terms of the run of the show, but the season of the nonprofit theatre. The number of performances of a particular production are predetermined by the theatre's season. For instance, the Slippery Rock University Theatre plans on four mainstage plays in its season, two in the spring and two in the fall. Like many other educational and nonprofit theatres, we share our space with numerous organizations such as the Dance and Music Department, the Performing Arts Series, and the Kaleidoscope Arts Festival. This means that even if a production is successful and there is a demand for more tickets to additional performances, we must close the production because of other scheduled events. Many nonprofit organizations find themselves in this position, and part of the responsibility of the managing director is to maximize the profit potential in the time available within the season.

Challenges of Producing Theatre

One of the major challenges facing all theatrical producing is the harsh reality of **cost disease**. Professional salaries determined by union negotiations continue to reflect the rising cost of living (and they should!). As they increase so do production expenses such as theatre rent and utilities, building materials for scenery and costumes, and equipment. Marketing costs such as advertising, programs, and promotional materials have also increased significantly in recent years.

COST DISEASE

A rise in labor costs without an increase in productivity. Originally studied for the performing arts sector by William J. Baumol and William G. Bowen. They observed that the same number of musicians are required to play a piece of classical music today as when it was composed in previous centuries, but the cost of compensating the musicians continues to increase.

Ticket sales generate substantial revenue for both commercial and nonprofit theatres. For nonprofits, the revenue from ticket sales provides evidence that the organization is meeting their mission and serving the public. In the commercial sector ticket sales indicate the demand for the property. However, all ticket sales are limited to the capacity of the theatre and the number of times that a production can be staged. Furthermore, the performing arts have the additional challenge of fixed costs in that the number of practitioners required for any production is largely predetermined. For example, the cast of the musical *Cats* must always include the number of characters that Andrew Lloyd Webber composed. A modest production of Shakespeare's *A Midsummer Night's Dream* still must include lovers, fairies, and mechanicals. While reducing the number of actors is often an artistic strategy, it is rarely a financial one.

In order to address the cost disease, producers and managing directors find strategies to raise revenue in other areas. Producers often turn to corporate sponsorship. Broadway theatre properties are particularly attractive to major sponsors. Managing directors increase revenue by securing grants and seeking donors from the public and private sectors.

Conclusion

Producing theatre is a challenging process in both the commercial and nonprofit sector. A producer must have a complete understanding of the value of theatre in terms of both its artistic and economic value. The process of creating a property, arranging for rehearsals and performances, supervising the marketing and sales, and managing the run can take a tremendous investment of time, money, and resources. However, producers reap the financial rewards as well as the satisfaction of bringing great art into the world. Managing directors secure the longevity of their nonprofit organizations and ensure that their practitioners will continue to have a place to perform. Producers make meaning in the theatre by creating the opportunities for theatre to happen in a challenging economic environment.

THE REHEARSAL PROCESS

Rebecca Morrice, Colleen Reilly, David Skeele, and Laura Smiley

CHAPTER OBJECTIVES

- Recognize that theatre is a collaborative process.
- Identify the steps in the rehearsal process.
- Understand the role of the stage manager in coordinating the rehearsal process.
- Understand the importance of communication in the rehearsal process.
- Recognize the rehearsal process as a culmination of theatre craft.

KEY TERMS

Cue to cue
Dress rehearsal
Stage manager
Strike
Technical rehearsal

The Director/Designer Relationship

Of the many tasks the modern director performs, the trickiest is perhaps the task of coordinating and helping synthesize the work of other theatre artists. On one hand, the director is responsible for making sure the various artistic elements mesh together and serve some kind of overall vision of the play. On the other, the director is collaborating with a host of individual artists who must be allowed the freedom to work their own magic on their specific areas of production.

Imagine you are a scene designer and a director approaches you with this vision for the play: "It's a play, I think, about...love. Not romantic love, exactly, although some of it is romantic. The set should be kind of modern, and it should be lyrical, but not too lyrical (except in places). We should see some of the cynicism of the world of the play. Oh yeah, and there should be some columns somewhere." What exactly could you do with this inarticulate nonsense? You would have to do a lot of guessing about what this director meant, and there would be good chance that your fellow designers would each have a different (possibly radically different) interpretation of what the words meant.

Now imagine the director says this: "I want two octagonal columns upstage, with a round revolving platform center. Surround the platform with scaffolding that has been spray-painted hot pink, and hang a giant, fringed yellow curtain behind the columns." Nothing vague here—this is much better, right? Of course not. Actually, it's much worse. What this director has done is essentially walked up to you and said: "Here's my set. Build it for me." Not only has this director completely stifled you creatively, he has taken over an area in which he is presumably far less skilled than you, and so assured himself an inferior set.

We've now seen examples of how not to communicate with designers, but we still haven't answered the question of how a good director/designer relationship functions.

Typically, a director meets with set, lighting, costume, properties, and sound designers long before the first rehearsal (hair and make-up designers, too, sometimes). The director has prepared for the meeting by doing exhaustive readings of the script and research on the time period, place, culture, and situations contained in the play, and at these early meetings, the designers are generally content to let the director do most of the talking. There are many avenues a director might wish to explore with the designers: the particular elements of the play he or she finds exciting and thus wishes to stress, what he or she feels the play is about, the images or feelings or moods the play seems to evoke. In conducting this discussion, the director generally tries to find a middle path between the two extremes described earlier. He or she wants to convey his or her interpretation as vividly and concretely as possible, but leave up to the designers most (if not all) decisions about how to translate these ideas into actual costumes and sets and soundscapes.

Sometimes, of course, a director's interpretation often already includes some sense of how the production might look or sound, but suggestions in this regard need not be overbearing or stifling to the designers. In fact, designers often appreciate "jumping-off points" for their own ideas, and they are almost always able to transform the director's suggestions so completely that there is no question of whose artistry is being featured. As a director, I like to think of it this way: I hand the designers some ideas, they wrestle with them for a while and then hand them back to me at least five times better than they were!

As an example, a few years ago I directed Slippery Rock University's production of *Oedipus Rex*. In my initial discussions with designers, I expressed to them my desire to go far away from the usual methods of producing collegiate Greek tragedy. No rows of robed people moaning and declaiming in unison for me, thanks. I felt that the most satisfying Greek tragedy I had ever seen had been done with puppets, so I suggested an approach in which each character would be a kind of life-sized puppet, voiced by a different actor who sat at a table upstage and spoke the lines into a microphone. I also wanted a setting for the play that effectively communicated the sense of the characters being larger than life. In this post-Watergate, post-Monica Lewinsky world, we no longer view political figures as being more than human. But if our leaders are no longer the god-like beings they were in ancient Greece, what kind of people do seem larger than life to us? Athletes, perhaps, and rock stars. My choice, though, was comic superheroes. I didn't want to be too obvious, with Oedipus in tights and a cape with a huge "O" emblazoned on his chest, but I did want to strongly suggest that mythical superhero world we all believed in so desperately as children. I suggested to the designers a world fashioned after D.C. Comics of the 1940s and '50s, and then stepped back and let them work their magic.

Set and lighting designer Gordon Phetteplace came up with a menacing urban skyscape, where cut-out buildings flared at the top in cartoonish forced perspective, and bathed it in the mysterious nighttime blues and greens that once covered the pages of Batman. Costume designer Jenny Bernson fashioned (as one example) a suit for the title character with wide lapels, impossibly broad and square shoulders and a sharply tapered waist, while his full-face mask featured a jutting, square jaw and Superman's trademark forehead curl. These designs originated in some way with my interpretive ideas, but I would have been almost completely incapable of turning those ideas into a living reality, and anything I might have managed would have paled before the exquisite craftsmanship and visual imagination of these skilled artists.

It is worth noting that the working methods I describe here are typical, but there are other models for director/designer collaboration. Sometimes, it is a particular designer who conceives of an initial production element, and then the director bases his or her work on that element. For instance, a costume designer may have an interest in working with a particular kind of fabric, or in designing in a particular period, and the director allows this fabric or this period to serve as his or her own jumping-off point. In educational theatre, it is sometimes desired by scene designers and technical directors that students have experience in building different kinds of sets. So a need for an arena staging might be accepted by the director as a given, and allowed to influence the overall interpretation of the play.

The exact collaborative model is not that important. What is important is that the process is collaborative. If there is open, clear, and honest communication, and if each artist respects the parts contributed by the others, the production stands a much greater chance of forming a coherent and powerful whole.

The Stage Manager

You are probably wondering how all of this process can come together with so many different practitioners and perspectives working toward the same goal. Have you ever heard the expression "there are too many cooks in the kitchen"? While the director is the final authority on the production, the expertise of each of the practitioners is mutually respected. In order to be sure that there is clear communication and organization of ideas it is absolutely necessary that a **stage manager** be in place throughout the rehearsal process.

The stage manager has the full responsibility for the execution of the production from its conception to its life on stage. They are present in preliminary meetings, at auditions, throughout the rehearsal process, and for every performance during a production run. This is because they must ensure that the vision of the director and designers is faithfully performed every time. The stage manager undertakes a variety of activities to successfully run smooth production meetings, rehearsals, and production meetings.

In my experience as a stage manager it is very important to be conscientious, organized, and good natured. You have to listen very closely to the concerns of the director, designers, and actors and work proactively towards a solution. This occurs in very small production scenarios such as when a prop is misplaced onstage, to serious personal issues like the replacement of an injured actor.

The stage manager takes detailed production notes during rehearsal and distributes them to everyone involved in the production staff. They collect cue sheets from each of the designers and assemble them into a master prompt book which also contains the production script. The promptbook is comprised of the cues, blocking, rehearsal schedules, contact information, ground plans, and numerous other essential documents for the production. It is often referred to as the production "bible."

A good stage manager is part referee, part nanny, and part prison warden. She must be able to keep lines of communication clear, nurture the artists involved in the process, and be very firm about deadlines, schedules, and expectations. With a stage manager in place the production staff can trust that they are working in a safe and controlled environment. The director and designers can be confident that their choices will be respected. And the actors are reassured that the things needed for their performance will be in place. The continuity that a stage manager brings to the rehearsal process allows everyone to be creative!

The Rehearsal Process

Rehearsal is a time of discovery! An intricate dance of give and take among the actor, the director, and the ensemble. Frequently the first rehearsal is the first time the director and the cast have been together. Introductions all around, business from the stage manager, words from the director and then...the first read-through. This is the first time that this play has been read with this particular group of actors for this particular production of the play. The first read-through is not about the acting, it is about listening—to the words, their rhythm and cadences, the voices of the ensemble, the story. After the read-through, there is table work: discussion and questioning about the text, the characters, the concept. This is where the foundation is laid.

I find table work especially crucial in doing Shakespeare. We look up words when we are not sure of their meaning, and literary, mythological, and geographical references. At this point the designers often join the table. The scene designer may bring a model, the costume designer renderings. This helps the actors visualize and actively imagine the world of the play, which helps them interpret and construct their characters. On a more practical level, it gives them an idea of how many steps it might take to cross the stage or climb the steps or what freedom or constraint their costumes allow. From here on, the process differs from director to director.

While the director and the actors are working on blocking and characterization in rehearsals, the designers and their teams are involved in the process of bringing their ideas to life as well. The designers continue to meet with the director, the stage manager keeps the designers and technicians informed of changes made during rehearsals, the designers collaborate with one another to make sure their work will mesh together, and the technicians are building in their respective shops.

During the production process, the costume designer will be making and finding costumes and scheduling fittings with the actors. The prop master will be providing rehearsal props for the actors to work with, while also making and finding the props that will be used in the actual performance. The technical director will be building the sets. While all of these activities may be happening in the same building or in separate locations across town, eventually everyone will come back together for *first tech* which is the *first technical rehearsal* when the set, lights, props, and sound are all integrated into the actors' and director's process.

Some theatre companies choose to introduce costumes at this time too; others will wait a few more days before actors "dress" for the first time. If they choose to wait to introduce the costumes, *first dress* will usually happen within a few days of first tech once the technical elements have been adjusted and set. For everyone, first dress is when finally begin to see and understand what the finished production will be like. It is a very exciting and exhausting process!

What is true to all rehearsal processes, is that it is a vital time of exploration and discovery necessary to bring the page to the stage in a creative fashion. As opening night approaches new elements are added during tech week. In these **technical rehearsals**, the lights, scenery, and sound cues become integrated.

Before an actual technical run, there is usually something called a **cue to cue**. This is the rehearsal when all the technical elements come together for the first time. The actors are asked to be patient as the designers and technical staff run the production literally from cue to cue: from one lighting cue to a sound cue to a scene change. It is during this time that sound and light levels are set and scene changes are choreographed. Once these aspects are in place, there will be several runs of the play with these components added to rehearse the calling of technical cues and for the actors to acclimate to these new elements. And then there are the **dress rehearsals**: this is when the actors wear their costumes for the first time. This completes the technical cycle of the rehearsal process. This is an exciting time for the actors—the costumes are the finishing touches of character development. It should be noted here that often during the rehearsal process, actors will be given rehearsal costumes to work with, especially if the play is a period piece. I frequently ask the costume designer for shoes for my actors—I find that shoes help with creating the physicality of the character. Think about it: you move quite differently depending on whether you are wearing sneakers or high heels or dress oxfords!

Depending on the production schedule, preview performances follow. This completes the circle, the final piece of the puzzle without which there would be no theatre: the audience! At this time, the audience is invited to experience the production before its scheduled opening. During these performances, adjustments are made to make the play more effective. It can be technical, for example raising or lowering the sound levels; or it can be about pacing and rhythm of the scenes. Very often, there are post-show discussions to elicit responses from the audience about what was effective and perhaps what was not. In any case it is a period during which adjustments can be made before the opening night when the critics arrive!

And finally it is here! This moment is the purpose of all the actor's training and the foundation built during the exhilarating and challenging rehearsal process. A well-rehearsed play provides the actor with the control and confidence to give a fully realized, totally energized performance. It provides the actor with the skills to be open to audience response as well as being able and prepared to adjust to any unexpected surprises that invariably happen in live performances. The final challenge once the play opens is for the actor to find ways to continually be true to the character and the world of the play, and to be fresh and in the moment whether the play runs for three days, three weeks, three months or three years!

The production **strike** is the final step in the rehearsal and production process. The set is disassembled and either destroyed or stored. Costumes are returned to stock or recycled. Props are stored, sound and lighting equipment disassembled, and scripts are returned to the publisher.

Conclusion

The rehearsal process is a dynamic time when all theatre practitioners engage in the process of making meaning in the theatre. This collaborative, deadline oriented, and creative process is one of the most unique features of theatrical art. As the process moves from auditions towards performance each participant is in constant communication about the work of bringing a unique performance to the stage through the dedicated efforts of everyone involved.

Exercises

Select a play mentioned in the course textbook and read it carefully.

Imagine that you are preparing a proposal for the production of this play. Your objective is to convince the reader to stage your production. Use citations from the text as needed to support your argument.

Prepare a one- to two-page analysis that must contain the following:

- Paragraph 1: A thesis statement that introduces your reasons for proposing the production.
- Paragraph 2: Describe the playwright's use of plot, character, and language.
- Paragraph 3: Identify the major character(s) and their objective(s).
- Paragraph 4: Create a concept for the production of the play from the viewpoint of a director.
- Paragraph 5: Provide a compelling and convincing conclusion to persuade the reader to stage your proposed production.